Praise for **From Stage Frig**

"*Whether you're a seasoned speaker or new to the speaking world, this book is an absolute must! This is the complete encyclopedia that every speaker needs to become a dynamic, charismatic and powerful speaker. Apply Steve's wisdom and watch as your speaking engagements explode!*"

> – Peggy McColl *New York Times* Best-Selling Author,
> www.Destinies.com

"*Want real how-to information about how to become a great speaker? Steve makes it easy with his direct, step-by-step approach. What a quick and easy way to become a great public speaker. I'm sure you'll enjoy his book as much as I did.*"

> – Tom "Big Al" Schreiter, www.BigAlReport.com

"*Steve Lowell's* **From Stage Fright to Spotlight** *takes the best thinking on modern communication along with his own experience, knowledge and common sense, and wraps it in an easy to digest must-read book for anyone who needs to quickly understand and practice the routes to great public speaking. I would certainly put it down as a book I wish I had written first!*"

> – Mark Bowden, author of *Winning Body Language*,
> www.Truthplane.com

"*Steve Lowell's book has pearls of wisdom that are not to be missed. The first two sections of the book alone are worth the price of the book. The thoughts on self-management and responsibility for outcome of the presentation are highly worthwhile, and the Appendix on the use of PowerPoint, including sections of the book dealing with it, are tremendously helpful with today's over-reliance on technology in place of creativity, substance and engagement with the audience. Every speaker who wants to improve his or her craft should read this book!*"

> – Louis B. Cady, MD, Founder, CEO, Cady Wellness Institute,
> www.Cadywellness.com

"Steve's new book, **From Stage Fright to Spotlight** encapsulates a wealth of wisdom. These are great strategies that are easy to understand and most importantly, easy to implement. What a terrific read for any professional speaker or for anyone that aspires to the craft."

> – Saul Jacobson, International Mentor/Master Presenter,
> Author of *He Made Me Think*,
> www.SaulJacobson.wordpress.com

"Brilliant! This book is a MUST read for anyone looking to speak in public professionally or otherwise. It is the most no-nonsense, down-to-earth and practical books I've ever read on this topic. Follow Steve Lowell's 99 tips and you will become the speaker you've always dreamed of."

> – Roslyn Franken, Speaker, Coach and Author of
> *The A List: 9 Guiding Principles for Healthy Eating and Positive Living*, www.roslynfranken.com

"Excellent book if you are really serious about becoming a better Speaker. Steve's book is very captivating and engages you all the way through bringing to light everything you wanted or needed to know to develop your speaking skills. I have heard Steve speak on numerous occasions and this book is like being there live and having your own personal coach guiding you step by step. Steve is an experienced and seasoned pro – his book is a must have!"

> – Elliott Smith, Professional Magician, Speaker and Author,
> www.seethemagic.com

Before you get started…
Steve has a message for you…

ZAP IT

Download the Zappar app
(or visit web.zappar.com)
and then scan this code to find the message.

READY
Download Zappar
for free from
the AppStore or
Google Play

ZAP
Aim at the
zapcode
and scan

LEARN
Watch images,
animations and
videos come to
life on the page!

FROM
STAGE FRIGHT
TO
SPOTLIGHT

99 Speakers' Secrets to
Breaking the Rules and Mastering the Stage

STEVE LOWELL

Published by
Hasmark Publishing
www.hasmarkpublishing.com

Permission should be addressed in writing to Steve Lowell at
steve@stevelowell.com

Edited by Nancy Slick & Rene Boucher

Cover & Book Design: Anne Karklins
anne@hasmarkpublishing.com

ISBN 13: 978-1-989756-10-2
ISBN 10: 1989756107

Hasmark
PUBLISHING
INTERNATIONAL

This book is dedicated to my amazing wife, Jayne.
Everything good that comes to me, comes from you first.
I am who I am and what I am because of what
you have helped me become.

TABLE OF CONTENTS

CHAPTER 3
TELL A COMPELLING STORY

CHAPTER 4
PREPARING TO MASTER THE STAGE

CHAPTER 5
PREPARING YOUR MIND FOR STAGE MASTERY

CHAPTER 6
PREPARING FOR A POWERFUL DELIVERY

CHAPTER 7
ARRIVING AT THE GIG

CHAPTER 8
JUST BEFORE SHOW TIME

CHAPTER 9
TAKE THE STAGE

CHAPTER 10
GAINING AND KEEPING MOMENTUM

CHAPTER 11
BEING SENSATIONAL

ACKNOWLEDGEMENTS

The first person I would like to acknowledge is my good friend, *New York Times* best selling author, Peggy McColl!

One day, while visiting her at her beautiful home, I mentioned to Peggy that I was writing a book about public speaking. She guided me and encouraged me every step of the way until the book was finally written.

Peggy has been an inspiration, a mentor and a precious friend.

Thank you to my parents, Jim and Eileen Lowell for always supporting me even though my career choices have been a little "off the wall," to say the least.

To my munchkin-head, Amanda; thanks for making me laugh and lending me your smiles when I was unable to find my own.

Thanks also to my best buddy, Dave (Bruce) Falle. When times got tough, you have always been there.

PREFACE

Think of the last time you saw a really engaging speaker who enthralled you with his or her message.

What was it about this speaker that captivated you? Was it the words the speaker said, the polished delivery or the way he or she made you feel?

There are three camps when it comes to speaking. The first camp comprises those who know and obey all the rules and present a highly polished delivery. The second camp contains those who know few or none of the rules and present a weak and fumbling delivery. Then there is a small population of those in the third group; those who know all the rules and then break them selectively and strategically. These are the speakers who know that in order to reach the audience at the emotional level they must do things differently than other speakers.

Throughout this book, I will share with you some common-sense rules, techniques and tactics for speaking in public, some hidden secrets that professional speakers use and some gems that I have picked up along the way that no-one else is likely to ever teach you. In all, there are 99 points in this book, some of which are profoundly simple, some just profound. Yet all of them combine to provide you with a solid foundation and understanding of the little things that make the big differences when speaking in public.

I will share with you the reasons behind the rules so that you can then decide for yourself which ones to break and how to break them because breaking a few rules well will give you complete command and control over the stage and help you to stand out as a speaker.

At the end of each chapter are some "Points to Ponder". I encourage you to take some time and reflect on these points and questions.

In keeping with the theme of breaking the rules, you may notice as you're reading that my grammar is not always perfect. You will likely notice some sentence structure errors and maybe the odd punctuation blunder. There are two reasons for this:

1. I have tried to write as I speak, and I asked my editors to make sure to keep my conversational style in tact as much as possible.

2. One of my editors, Nancy, told me that if we sterilized the writing too much it would read more like a university textbook for speech 101. This book is really meant for the guy or lady on the plane who has to do a presentation in a few hours and is scared to death. She told me that after reading this book the reader kind of feels like going for a beer with me and "hangin out". That's the reaction I was looking for! So, after reading this book, if you would like to buy me a beer and hang out, I'm down for that!

Now, if you're ready to find out the secrets to how you can command the stage by learning and then breaking a few rules, let's get moving!

CHAPTER 1

NINE SPEAKING MYTHS
TO CLEAR UP RIGHT NOW!

#1
Myth One – FEAR =
"False Evidence Appearing Real"

Many of us have heard that the word FEAR is really nothing more than an acronym for "False Evidence Appearing Real." Many motivational speakers and personal development-types use this definition to remind us that the things we fear the most are usually not worthy of the emotional baggage we tend to attach to them.

I believe this definition of the word FEAR holds merit in the business of day to day living. You have probably been in situations where you create the worst-case scenario in your head and project that scenario as the most probable outcome of the situation. Then you attach the associated emotional baggage to that outcome and let that baggage drive the way you respond to the other things that happen in your life.

When the situation does finally resolve itself, you discover the scenario you created in your mind did not materialize. The outcome was not nearly as bad as you anticipated. Certainly, it was not worthy of the emotional baggage you attached to it. Worse still, you were living your life based on a scenario that never evolved. For that entire time, your life was driven by the emotional baggage that was attached to an outcome based on *false evidence that only appeared to be real.*

There are situations, however, when fear isn't based on false evidence that only appears to be real. Worst-case scenarios may be the most likely outcome at times. That outcome is worthy of the emotional baggage we may attach to it and is based on a different "FEAR," namely, "Factual Evidence that's Absolutely Real."

Let's consider a soldier in the streets of a war-torn city who is sent to the location of an explosive device. His job is to disarm that bomb. It doesn't take much imagination to determine the worst-case scenario here. I'm sure most soldiers in this situation would agree that a possible outcome is likely to be a worst-case scenario, and that outcome is worthy of all the emotional baggage a soldier might attach to it. Now, if that soldier treats the bomb as false evidence that only appears to be real, well, I suspect that's a mistake that would only be made once.

There are some people who consider the endeavor of public speaking isn't quite as dangerous as disarming a live bomb. I would tend to agree. However, I can tell you that I have seen many presentations blow up in the speaker's face, and the results can be devastating.

You may have heard that the fear of speaking in public is greater than the fear of death. I have never seen actual studies to support that claim. While it may well be that, statistically, most people would rather die than speak in public, I believe that most of us would agree that the fear of speaking in public is a substantial fear. Actually, most of us share this fear with varying degrees of intensity.

So, what is it that most people are afraid of when it comes to speaking in public? When I ask my students this question, the most common replies given include:

- What if I forget my words and look foolish?
- What if my audience doesn't like me?
- What if my audience doesn't believe me?
- What if I say the wrong thing and offend my audience?
- What if my audience judges me or criticizes me?
- What if everything goes wrong?

Essentially, the fear of speaking in public boils down to the fear of losing one's self-image, reputation and credibility.

Here's the truth about speaking in public: Every time you stand in front of an audience, your credibility, reputation and, thus your self-image, are on the line. Chances are high that you will forget something you had planned to say. It's highly possible that you will do or say something to offend people or, at the very least, cause them to disagree with you. Not everyone will believe you and most likely something will go wrong.

Why do I make this point? Because if you, as a speaker, treat the fear of speaking as "false evidence only appearing to be real," you will be less likely to put forth the effort required to reduce the likelihood of the worst-case scenario becoming the actual outcome. Your chances of incurring damage to your reputation, credibility and image become, in fact, very high.

The fear of public speaking isn't based on false evidence that only appears to be real, but it's based on *Factual Evidence that's Absolutely Real.*

The good news is that you hold in your hands the means by which you can substantially reduce the likelihood of the worst-case scenario manifesting itself into the probable outcome. In fact, by using the lessons in this book, the more likely outcome of your speaking endeavors will be to greatly enhance your reputation, credibility and thus, your image.

What's the lesson? The consequences of speaking poorly are real. Know the perils; respect the perils and prepare for the perils.

#2
Myth Two – The Fear Is All in My Head

What happens to you when it's your turn to speak in public? Do your hands shake? Does your pulse race? Does your blood pressure rise? For most of us the answers to these and other physical manifestations would be a resounding "YES!"

In his book, *Brain Rules*, Dr. John Medina explains what happens in your body when you're stressed. He explains that when you're faced with a stressful situation, either positive or negative, a structure in your brain called the hypothalamus reacts to the stress and sends a signal to your adrenal glands, which immediately dumps loads of adrenaline into your bloodstream, triggering what is known as the fight or flight response.

When adrenaline enters your system, it helps the fight or flight response by boosting your heart rate and increasing your breathing rate. This reaction allows more oxygen to course through your body so that a lot of energy is available when needed. Your pupils dilate to improve your vision, and most of the blood supply is directed to the skeletal muscles that help you run or fight, all the while restricting blood flow to your gut and skin by constricting blood vessels to these areas.

This all means that the fear of speaking isn't just in your head. It affects your entire physical being and alters the way you present yourself when you finally take the stage.

The fear of speaking isn't something you can talk yourself out of. It's something to be acknowledged, respected and dealt with properly. When dealt with properly, you can leverage the natural physical results associated with the fight or flight response into a powerful tool to help you be sensational when you speak.

As you prepare to take the stage at your next opportunity, remember that the fear you feel is real. It has physical manifestations and you must face them, acknowledge them and deal with them.

So, what's the lesson? Never try to talk yourself out of the fear or the anxiety. It will only frustrate you when you take the stage and that will make matters worse.

#3
Myth Three – Great Speakers Don't Get Stage Fright

Mark Twain once said "There are two types of speakers: those that are nervous and those that are liars."

Here's the truth about stage fright: everyone gets it to some degree. Now, having said that, I can tell you that there have been times when I have taken the stage as a performer with zero anxiety and I am not proud of that fact. Years ago, when I was playing music in bars for a living, there were nights when taking the stage meant no more to me than a job to make money and I did it because that's what I was hired to do.

On some of those late nights in lonely pubs with a handful of very intoxicated patrons, I felt no stage fright when I took the stage. That made me realize it was time for me to get out of that business, and I did. However, I can't remember a single time when I took the stage to speak without having some measure of fear.

Some speakers show no sign of fear, that's true. That's because those speakers have learned to acknowledge the fear, respect it and turn it into a constructive energy so what they feel drives them toward a better performance. They prepare so thoroughly, and they know the techniques so well, that they feel excitement more than fear. As a speaker, you want that fear and excitement. You need that fear and excitement because if you don't have it, you're probably taking the stage only for the money, because that's what you have been hired to do, and that could mean it's time to get out of the business.

Why is this important to you? Because you need to know that when your hands shake, when your pulse races and when your blood pressure rises, that's precisely what's supposed to happen! If these things don't happen, it means that you're not emotionally involved and you should think twice about taking the stage. A lack of emotional involvement likely means a lack of respect for the opportunity, leading to poor preparation and thus right back to the first myth. Therefore, "FEAR," in regards to public speaking, doesn't equal false evidence appearing real. Rather, the fear of speaking in public is based on factual evidence that's absolutely real. That fear will drive proper preparation, which will translate to sensational performances resulting in the best possible outcome.

So, what's the lesson? Love that fear, you need it!

#4
Myth Four – There Is No "Right Way" To Do It

I have heard many speech coaches state that "there is no right or wrong way to speak in public," and I completely disagree! I believe that there is a right and a wrong way and, if you do it the wrong way, it could all explode in your face.

I have seen speech coaches train their clients to keep their hands down by their sides, to limit their pacing, to slow themselves down and to make sure their tie is straight. In most cases, paying attention to these things is the exact wrong way to do it, and let me tell you why.

If you're speaking in public, you probably have something valuable to say. More than that, you believe you have a message that needs to be shared or a story that needs to be told. You want to be the catalyst for a change you feel driven to make in this world. As a speaker, if you're emotionally involved in your message, if you believe in your message and its importance to your audience, the right way to deliver that message is whatever way gets you the desired result. The desired result will come from your heart, not your tie.

In 2009, a friend of mine sent me an audio clip of a speech he gave at a major speaking club event for which he was awarded very high marks. He did it the "right way" according to his speaking club. When I listened to the audio clip, I remember thinking how perfect his delivery was. He was articulate, with no "ums" or "ahs." His speech was well organized, his speed and volume changed in all the right places and his delivery was polished and flawless, like that of a machine. I have no clue what his message was, because his delivery was so mechanical that there was absolutely no emotional involvement. There was no "human element" to his speech. Because there was no emotional involvement on his side, there was none on mine, and his message was, therefore, not worthy of capturing my attention. Now, that was not a conscious thought at the time, but that's the reason I don't remember his message. We do not pay attention to boring things.

His speech was simply transference of information. But speaking should not simply be transference of information; it should be transference of feelings as well. If I can make you feel the same way about my topic as I do, then we understand each other.

Throughout this book, we'll explore tips and techniques that will allow you to speak authentically. These tips and techniques are not designed to turn you into something you're not as you orate on stage; they're designed to help bring out more of the real you. In my workshops, I spend an enormous amount of time helping people let go of rules they have been taught about speaking, and teach them to be themselves. Then, we apply the proper techniques in accordance with their own personality to help them bring out more of who they really are.

So, what's the lesson? When you're speaking, be authentic, get lost in your message and let the real you shine through. That's the right way to do it.

#5
Myth Five – Great Speakers Can Just Wing It

This has to be the most dangerous myth of all. The danger isn't in thinking that other speakers can wing it, the danger is in thinking that you can.

Here's the truth about winging it: Even the pros can't really do it well!

A professional speaker is the same as any other professional. They're so well prepared that they make it look effortless. It seems they can stand up and speak at any time, under any circumstances, and most of them can, only if they're prepared. Remember that being prepared has nothing to do with memorizing your presentation; it has to do with knowing your message so well that you can speak about it at any time.

I shudder when I hear someone tell me they have a presentation to give and they're just going to wing it. I have suffered through countless presentations and speeches that were off the cuff and I can tell you that I have never, ever seen a presenter "wing it" and give a truly good presentation.

Tiger Woods may be able pick up a golf club at any time and play a great game of golf with no prior notice, but does that mean he's winging it? No, because Tiger is a professional and his countless hours of practice make him prepared.

As a speaker, you need to know your material so well that you're always prepared to speak about it, even at a moment's notice. What may seem like winging it turns out to be efficient preparation.

Many speakers confuse polite feedback from their audience with having given a good presentation. Here's a secret you need to know: people will always tell you what a great job you did, even if you suck! As a speaker, what you care about isn't what your audience says to you, but how they feel about you and your message.

When you wing it, even though you may feel good about your performance and your audience may give you kind feedback, it's likely that many more of your audience noticed your lack of preparation and feel a little ripped off. After all, they invested their time to be there and you should have either invested the time to prepare or declined the invitation to speak.

So, what's the lesson? Even if you think you can wing it, you probably can't. Be prepared at all times.

#6
Myth Six – I Have Nothing Important to Say

Everyone has a story to tell, a story that could change lives. The unfortunate part is that most of these stories will never be heard, because most people either think that their story isn't important, or they just don't have the skill or confidence they need to stand up and speak in front of an audience to bring their story to life.

Everyone has had successes, failures, victories and challenges. Everyone has been happy, sad, hurt and angered. All you need to do is find the wisdom in the lessons you have gained from your life experience and share them with the world. Each of our journeys is unique, never before seen and never to be repeated. Start thinking of your daily activities as a series of lessons, and you will see that you have a wealth of information to share with this world. The world needs to hear your story, and we need to hear it from you.

In chapter three, we'll discuss how to find the profound in the mundane, by finding life lessons in everyday events to which most people pay little attention. There are lessons all around you, every single day, and these are lessons you can share with others, lessons that could change lives.

Zig Ziglar once said, "You are who you're and where you're because of what has gone into your mind." To find your story, take stock of where you are in your life, and of the person you have become. What events have transpired in your life that molded your character and beliefs? What teachers have influenced you during your life, and what lessons did they teach you? What successes or failures have you experienced, and what did you learn from them?

Each one of us has a lifetime of lessons to share, and the best way to share your life is in your own words. People want to hear your story. They want to know what you know and how you learned it.

So, what's the lesson? You have a lifetime of lessons to share so don't be afraid to share them.

#7
Myth Seven – I Have to Be Funny So That People Like Me

Have you ever seen someone speaking in public who tries hard to be funny, but just can't seem to make it work? Painful, isn't it?

Some people have the ability to use humor effectively in their speeches, and that's just great, but most of us don't have that particular skill.

I know a lady who's highly intelligent, very successful and widely respected in the business community. She has truckloads of wisdom and insights to share with the world, but, every time she takes the stage, she tries to lighten the mood by making little wisecracks and jokes. These are the result of nothing more than nervous energy finding its way out through bad attempts at jest.

Once she gets on a roll, she has magnificent things to say, but getting out of the gate is very difficult for her, because she needs time to "ramp up." During that ramping up period, her attempts at humor are very uncomfortable for her and the audience, because they're perceived as awkward moments of tremendous nervousness, which is precisely what they are.

The problem with using humor as a warm-up to your presentation is that your audience dictates the result. If your humor is a hit and the audience laughs, you're going to feel great about it and it will help you going forward, but if your humor doesn't hit the mark and the audience doesn't laugh, the effect on your confidence can be crippling and it can destroy your entire presentation.

Here's a little secret for you: your audience doesn't care if you're funny or not. A confident and emotionally sincere approach is always more effective than an awkward attempt at ineffective humor.

Humor can be a nice little bonus for your audience, but unless you're branding yourself as a comedian, humor isn't expected and isn't required. Your audience wants to get to know the real you, and if humor isn't part of the real you, don't force it.

So, what's the lesson? Humor is a tremendous tool when used effectively, but it's not a requirement and should be used only by those who can do so naturally. We'll explore this further in chapter eleven.

#8
Myth Eight – I Could Never Be A Great Public Speaker

There are three things that stop someone from being a great public speaker: lack of skill, lack of confidence and lack of experience. Each one of these roadblocks is surmountable.

The skills to be a great speaker can be taught to anyone who's willing to learn. It's not always easy, but it can be done. Once a little skill is developed and the person begins to see and feel results, confidence begins to increase and they become more mindful of opportunities to speak up. This gives them added experience, which, in turn, gives them more opportunity to develop their skill. Soon, they begin trying out new techniques, expanding their comfort zone and becoming more relaxed and open in front of an audience.

The best speakers are not the ones who deliver the most polished performance. The best speakers are those who can move their audiences emotionally, and that's done by connecting with their audience at an emotional level. The more you show your audience the real you, the more impactful you will be as a speaker. Since anyone can learn to just be him or herself, anyone can learn to be a great speaker.

I have seen unpolished speakers with poor vocabulary and a less than attractive appearance completely captivate and move an audience more than some of the most professional and polished speakers with all the charisma in the known universe.

Yes, polish can be good, charisma is an asset and a pleasant appearance sure helps, but none of that's a pre-requisite for being a great speaker. The keys are openness, sincerity and passion for your topic. That passion, if great enough, will supersede any short-comings you may think you have. A speaker who can make an audience feel the way he or she feels about the topic at hand is a sensational speaker. Even if you weren't born with the "gift of gab," you can become a great speaker. All you have to do is gain a little skill, increase your confidence and add experience through practice.

So, what's the lesson? Show your passion and be yourself, you can be a great speaker.

#9
Myth Nine – A Great PowerPoint Presentation Is All I Need

We've all endured it at one time or another. In business today, it's virtually impossible to escape from. It's the scourge of the stage, the plague of the presentation and the blight of the business meeting. It's, "death by PowerPoint!"

In my judgment, presentation software such as PowerPoint is the worst thing to ever happen to the business of public speaking. The reason is that too many people use their presentation slides as a crutch. They spend far more time preparing bullet-point slides than they do preparing their own delivery, and a bullet-point slide can be prepared in less than sixty seconds.

Presentation software can be a very powerful tool. When used correctly, it can add sizzle, sparkle and power to your presentation. The problem is that maybe one in one-hundred presenters use the tool effectively.

In Chapter Six, we'll explore some techniques you can use to avoid "death by PowerPoint" and really make effective use of presentation software. The bottom line is this: presentation slides are meant to enhance your presentation, not replace you as the presenter. Do take the time to learn how to create great slides but always use them as a supporting tool only, not as the focal point of the presentation.

So, what's the lesson? A natural and engaging speaker is more captivating to an audience than a great PowerPoint presentation any day of the week!

Points to Ponder

1. Which myth(s) have you bought into?

2. How will your new understanding improve your next presentation?

CHAPTER 2

THE SPICE FORMULA OF SENSATIONAL SPEAKING

#10
S Is For Simplify

There's an organization in Canada that presents business seminars around the country on a regular basis. I attended several of these because a good friend of mine was presenting those sessions. At each session, the amount of material covered was so detailed that no one ever really received any value from it.

This was not the fault of the presenter. The presenter was actually a reasonably decent speaker, but he was bound to the presentation materials provided by the company.

Those business presentations were so saturated with facts, figures, ideas and concepts that it was impossible for anyone to remain attentive for the entire sixty to ninety minutes. By the end of each session, the entire audience was blurry-eyed and had learned very little, if anything at all.

That's how most presentations are—overloaded with details supporting far too many points.

So, what's the lesson? Simplify your presentation and your audience will learn far more.

#11
Gist Before Details

In his powerful book, *Brain Rules*, John Medena explains how research shows that the human brain records and recalls the gist of an event but doesn't record and recall a lot of the details. This means an audience will not likely remember much of a presentation about the two-hundred-thirty-seven steps to a successful marketing campaign.

On the other hand, if the presentation listed "The Three Top Marketing Strategies that Always Work" (gist), and then went on to support each of the three points with some relevant data (details), the audience would be more likely to get the point. They would remember the gist even if they don't recall all the details.

Here is a beautiful example of how simplifying the presentation can make all the difference in the world.

In the mid 1990's, I was working for a man who has since become my long-time mentor and friend, Anil Agrawal. Anil also happens to be one of the most intelligent people I have ever known, and to this day he remains my close friend.

I remember sitting at Anil's desk, across from him, with three information packets in front of me—a pink one, a blue one and a green one. Each of these packets contained the details of a different training program that we were selling at our company. My job was to learn the contents of the information packets and present these programs to clients.

The training programs were for people who were trying to break into the information technology business, and they were very complex and detailed training programs. Not having been in the information technology business myself, the concepts contained in these programs were well beyond my comprehension.

After a week of studying these information packets, I had many questions for Anil. As I proceeded to ask my questions, Anil was able to deduce that I didn't really understand the programs at all.

Even after a full week of reading and studying, my understanding of the material contained in those information packets was weak, to say the least.

Anil took a piece of paper and a pen, and proceeded to draw a triangle. He then drew two horizontal lines cutting the triangle into three parts.

Holding up the pink information sheets, he explained that this course was for a group of people called "end users," and he wrote "End Users" in the bottom section of the triangle. End users are the people who use computers every day and have knowledge of the application packages, but typically don't require any technical knowledge or knowledge of networks.

Then, Anil held up the blue information sheets. As he wrote "Power Users" in the middle section of the triangle, he explained that this course was for people who are more advanced computer users, have some semi-technical functions to perform in their work and have basic understanding of networks.

Holding up the green papers, Anil then wrote "Technical Users" in the top section of the triangle. He explained that this course was for advanced computer users in highly technical positions. These are the people who design, install and administer networks at companies.

After an entire week of studying the material and coming out with little or no understanding of the material, Anil brought it all together for me in less than five minutes by simplifying it to a level that I could understand. He presented the gist of the material, which prepared me to then go on and understand the details.

During the next few years, I went on to use that same diagram in my presentations to hundreds of people while I was out promoting and marketing our courses. As a result of these presentations, we generated several million dollars in business.

So, what's the lesson? Know that your audience is generally not interested in the fine details. Give them the big picture.

#12
P Is for Personalize

In early 2010, a nice English lady named Julia came to see me and wanted help overcoming her fear of speaking in public. She was in her forties and was an individual so uncomfortable when speaking in public that even standing up and giving her name was difficult for her.

I encouraged her to attend my eight-week course called "The Creating Confidence Course," which she did. In the fifth session of the course, Julia was giving her assigned talk. I watched the reactions of the class members, and I could clearly see that Julia had the undivided attention of every other student in the class. She had succeeded in getting the entire class in the palm of her hand.

Her two-minute talk included a personal story that captured the imagination of the entire audience. A few months later, I called Julia and told her I was giving a presentation about using personal examples while speaking, and I asked for her permission to use her speech to the class that day as an example. Julia graciously offered to come and give that talk herself, so I was thrilled to have her join me for my presentation.

I began the presentation by addressing the audience, who were numbering around seventy-five, and telling them about the power of including a personal story in a speech, and when the appropriate time came, I introduced Julia.

Now, an audience of seventy-five people isn't a large audience for some speakers, but for Julia it was huge!

Julia walked up to the front of the room and began to speak. In less than one full minute, Julia explained how she was sitting in a hair salon looking at her image in the mirror and feeling like it was the worst day of her life.

She went on to explain that she had recently lost her hair.

"Not some of my hair." Julia explained, "ALL of my hair!" And with those words, Julia reached up and pulled off her wig and stood before the entire room completely bald.

She then went on to explain how she has learned to accept, to live with and even to honor her illness.

At the conclusion of her speech, she briefly turned away from the audience to place her wig back on her head. As she turned to face the audience again, she had to bring her hands up to her face and she wept with surprise at the standing ovation she had elicited from a speech that had lasted less than one minute.

Julia could have spoken about the illness. She could have told the audience about the statistics, the cause of the illness, the treatments and all of the other available information about the illness. Instead, she chose to provide a personal example of her own experience in dealing with the illness and, as a result, she provided more than a speech. She provided a one-minute experience that no one in that room will soon forget!

That's the power of a personal story!

Of course, not all of us have as profound a story to tell as Julia's, but that doesn't mean we don't have a story to tell which can profoundly affect our audience.

Personal stories are like glue to a speech or presentation, if the stories are well told. They bind the pieces together and give your audience some points of reference to make the material relevant to their own lives. They also provide you with evidence that supports your qualification to speak about the topic.

So, what's the lesson? A well-told personal account that's relevant to the topic being covered can add tremendous value and impact to your speech.

#13
I Is For Intermittent Incongruity

The best way to explain this concept is with an example.

In late 2009, I was at a small networking meeting in Ottawa that featured Katrina as the guest speaker. Katrina is a family lawyer, and is a very pretty young lady, and she is a regular member of the group. Being a new member myself, I hadn't had the opportunity to speak with her much, so I didn't really know her well.

This group's intentions are to hold presentations that help members better understand each other's businesses, enabling everyone to refer business to each other through this networking.

During her presentation, Katrina stood behind a long table. At one end of this table, she placed two file folders along with a white banker's box, and at the other end she placed a sealed garment bag.

I noticed that Katrina was impeccably dressed. She was wearing a white blouse and scarf with a dark jacket and dress pants, so I wondered what the garment bag contained at the other end of the table.

She began her presentation with this statement. "There are four stages to the process of litigation for divorce." She then began to describe a situation that had occurred with a client of hers. Of course, the example was real, but the identities of the parties involved were never disclosed.

Katrina explained a bit about the situation, and within less than a minute, she held up the first file folder, containing a stack of papers about three inches thick. She slammed the file folder on the table in front of her and said, "This case was settled at stage one, 'negotiation.' This represents about five-thousand dollars in legal fees."

With her next words, Katrina began to unbutton her jacket. As you can imagine, this move perked up the attention of everyone in the room. *"Why is she unbuttoning her jacket?"*

With her jacket now unbuttoned, she began to describe a second case which went beyond the first stage of negotiation and into the second stage, called "mediation."

While she explained the mediation stage, Katrina held up the second file folder which was much thicker than the first. She slammed that folder on top of the first folder, and said "This is stage two. This represents about ten-thousand dollars in legal fees."

Katrina then moved to a third scenario in which the parties weren't able to settle in stage one or stage two and had to move into stage three, "arbitration." As she spoke, she removed her jacket, untied the scarf that was around her neck and removed that as well. Now she really had everyone's attention!

While this was happening, I thought to myself "I see what she's going to do here. She's going to take those clothes off and put whatever is in the garment bag on. I'm curious to see what happens between stage three and stage four!" Katrina had my undivided attention!

With her jacket and scarf now removed, Katrina stood there, wearing a white blouse with the top button or two unfastened. Although this wasn't an unusual state of dress for a professional woman, it was a stark contrast to her fully-covered appearance when she began her presentation only a few minutes earlier. Katrina continued to walk us through this interesting series of events.

Reaching into the banker's box this time, she retrieved several piles of paper and slammed each of the piles onto the table. She explained that the entire contents in this banker's box were generated by only one case, a case that had gone into the third stage. That paperwork represented about twenty-thousand dollars in legal fees.

Next, moving toward the garment bag, she explained that this particular client was not willing to settle, so they were going to move into stage four, "court proceedings."

While explaining stage four, Katrina extracted an accessory of clothing from the garment bag and placed the accessory around her neck, forming a collar. She then proceeded to do up the top buttons of her blouse. Her next move was the punch-line of her presentation.

Reaching into her garment bag, Katrina pulled out a black gown. This is the gown that she wore whenever she had to represent a client in court. In Canada, lawyers must wear a proper gown when in court. She placed the gown around her shoulders and, with perfect timing, she said, "Stage four is when the gown goes on, and when the gown goes on, the gloves come off!"

With that, she ended her presentation.

Before writing these words, I e-mailed Katrina to ask her permission to use her presentation as an example in this book. I had to ask her to remind me of a few details of her presentation, in order to give an accurate account here. I realized I had forgotten the names of the stages; I wasn't sure if there were four or five stages, and I couldn't recall what the dollar amounts attached to each stage of the process were, but, I certainly remembered the gist! I also remembered that in a divorce, every stage costs thousands of dollars more and divorces had better get done before the gown goes on, because when the gown goes on, the gloves come off!

You see, the brain likes gist more than details, and with Katrina's presentation, her details supported the gist. If we were to ask anyone who attended that presentation, my guess is that most of them wouldn't remember the exact details, but all of them would remember the gist. Mission accomplished!

According to Dr. John Medina, the human brain is a pattern recognition machine. Our brain likes to be able to predict with reasonable accuracy what is going to happen next, so we unconsciously scour the sensory landscape trying to find patterns.

We do this so that our brain doesn't have to process everything from scratch every time we experience sensory input. If our brain can predict the likely outcome by basing its expectations on a recognized pattern, it can relax and dedicate its neuro-processing energy to other things. When the outcome matches the expectation, that's congruity.

So, let's see how congruity was used by Katrina's presentation.

Katrina started her presentation, and as she spoke, my brain was searching for patterns. My brain identified a well-dressed lawyer at a table. The table held files and a banker's box on it, as well as a garment bag. This represented a pattern that helped me reasonably predict the outcome; Katrina was going to speak to us and reference those files, the banker's box and the garment bag.

In addition, my brain expects the pattern that people remain clothed as they give a presentation. That's the most recognized pattern, so the expected outcome was that Katrina would remain clothed during her presentation.

Another pattern emerged as Katrina slammed the first file folder on the table and announced, "This represents about five-thousand dollars in legal fees." My brain set the expectation that each time she referenced those papers, there would be a dollar amount attached to it.

Then, Katrina did something profound—she violated the expectation of an existing pattern. By unbuttoning her jacket, Katrina breached the pattern that predicted she would remain clothed during her presentation.

While Katrina unbuttoned her jacket, my brain said, "Hey! What's this? This isn't congruent with the predicted outcome of this recognized pattern!" This is an intermittent incongruity.

So my brain was in a bit of a conundrum because it began questioning the predicted outcome of a previously established pattern, and it became more alert as it entered a stage of dissonance. My brain needed to establish whether or not there was a new pattern emerging so it could predict the outcome. My brain was not relaxed!

While Katrina continued with her presentation, my brain was not only scouring the environment for a new pattern, but it was also reconfirming the other known patterns to ensure that they had not also been breached. Katrina had my full attention!

When Katrina removed her scarf, a new pattern was recognized and a new expectation was set—Katrina was going to disrobe during the presentation! But wait! There's a garment bag there. That was another element of the pattern, so not only was she going to disrobe, she was going to put on a new set of clothes. The pattern had been confirmed, the outcome had been predicted and the expectation had been set. But there's a problem. The pattern had a gap. What was going to happen between the time she took her existing clothes off and put the replacement clothes on? Once again, my brain searched for patterns to predict that outcome.

When Katrina first reached into the garment bag and donned the collar, she again breached an identified pattern and violated the predicted outcome. My brain had predicted that she was going to take one set of clothes off and then put another set of clothes on, but she didn't do that. She began putting the second set of clothes on without taking the entire first set of clothes off. This was incongruent with the pattern and presented another intermittent incongruity.

Now, you might be saying "you didn't actually think that she was going to completely disrobe in front of the entire room, did you?" Well, I am a man, and we do tend to think that way! However, I was not consciously expecting her to disrobe in front of everyone in the room. On an unconscious level, though, my brain predicted the outcome of a change of clothes. How it was going to be accomplished was the gap in the pattern due to the environment.

If I watched Katrina walk into a change-room with a garment bag, the predicted outcome based on that pattern would be that she would remove one set of clothes before donning the other set of clothes. That's an expected outcome predicated by the recognized pattern of going into a change room while carrying a change of clothes.

But, in front of an audience, there was a gap in the pattern. I could see what she was wearing, I could see what appeared to be a change of clothes, but the environment was wrong. The environment was not congruent with the other two parts of the pattern. This posed an intermittent incongruity.

Katrina's presentation was filled with patterns and predictable outcomes, but she inserted just enough intermittent incongruities to keep my brain searching for patterns and trying to predict what was going to happen next. She had my full attention every second of her presentation.

But there's more!

When an incongruity occurs, the brain is sparked to a state of alertness, and during those split seconds, it's able to receive and retain more information because it's looking for answers. So, Katrina not only kept my brain awake, she also created an environment where I could accept the information she was presenting.

So, what's the lesson? When possible, insert a slight but relevant intermittent incongruity into your presentation to maintain interest.

#14
C Is For Confident Delivery

In 2008, Hilke Plassman, associate professor of marketing at INSEAD Business School near Paris, conducted an experiment on wine connoisseurs whereby he placed false price tags on bottles of the same Cabernet Sauvignon. In this blind taste test, some of the bottles of wine appeared to be priced at $10, while other bottles were listed at $90. Volunteers, who were unaware of the experiment, proceeded to give a considerably higher rating to the $90 bottles of wine than to the $10 bottles, even though they both contained the exact same wine.

But, it doesn't stop there. During a functional MRI scan, Plassman discovered there was a difference in the neural activity deep within the brain when the volunteers drank the wine. Not only did the "cheaper" wine taste cheaper to the volunteers, the pricier wine generated increased activity in the medial orbitofrontal cortex, the part of the brain that responds to pleasurable experiences.

So what does this have to do with public speaking? Everything!

Fairly or not, your audience is going to pass an initial judgment on you the second you walk onto that stage, and this initial judgment of you will reflect on the posture with which you take to that stage. If you present yourself as a $90 bottle of fine wine, you'll be perceived as such by your audience. If you present yourself as a $10 bottle of cheap table wine, well, I think you get the point.

You've probably been told that even though you may feel self-conscious and nervous when you give a speech, your audience can't always tell you're nervous unless you give it away somehow. That's generally the case, and, unless you make it obvious to them, your audience will not usually detect your nervousness. However, what they can always detect is a healthy sense of confidence. Your audience can detect it, and they like it, even at the neurological level.

One student in my training program was very shy and timid when she spoke before an audience, but she was not nearly as shy when speaking one-on-one in normal conversation. She told me she felt that it was improper to appear too confident while speaking in public because she felt her audience would perceive her as being conceited. The problem was that her audience had a difficult time accepting her as a trusted source because she appeared to have little confidence in herself and in her message.

Conceit and confidence are not the same thing. Conceit is a strange disease; it makes everyone sick except the one who has it. When I talk about confidence, I'm not talking about an over-inflated, "I am the greatest" ego, I'm talking about a healthy self-image and a solid belief in your message and your ability to deliver it. So the question is, how does one build that level of confidence? Well, there are three ways you can position yourself to help you gain the confidence you need as a public speaker. The three ways to position yourself are: As an expert, as a reporter and as a philosopher. Each of these positions is covered by the next three points, respectively.

So, what's the lesson? The exact same wine can taste different if it's presented in a $90 bottle of wine and a $10 bottle of wine.

#15
Be an Expert Who Speaks

There's an old adage in the speaking business that says "Don't be a speaker, be an expert who speaks." An expert is someone who speaks from wisdom. Wisdom is simply knowledge gained from experience. If you have personally experienced something in your life, you have earned the right to speak about it.

In Chapter Three, we'll discuss finding the profundity in the mundane. This basically means you can extract value from just about every daily event that you experience and turn it into a lesson. This qualifies you as an expert on that specific lesson, since you're able to validate the point with personal wisdom.

Years ago when I was with a previous life partner, she and I would do seminars and speaking engagements about the experiences we dealt with regarding her depression and emotional illness. She and I both went through hell and back dealing with her depression and all of the associated illness and behavior that goes with it.

When she and I spoke about her illness and how we dealt with it, she will open up her heart and share her deepest and darkest thoughts about her former behavior. She would say she stands "figuratively naked" before her audience to help them understand exactly what goes through the mind of someone who suffers from this illness.

I did the same, but my expertise was gained from the other side of the coin, being the person facing the challenges that present themselves when your life is intertwined with someone afflicted by depression. I shared the trials that I endured at the hands of her illness and, together, we shared what worked for us, and what didn't work for us.

Do these experiences qualify us as experts on the subject of depression? No, we were not experts on the subject of depression, but, we were experts on how to deal with HER depression, having found the combination of treatments that works for us through trial and error. This meant that when we spoke, our audience regarded us as experts in dealing with depression, since we had lived the every-day life of those who suffer because of depression, and how it affects their families.

We spoke from experience, since we had lived through it ourselves and we had earned the right to speak about it. This experience provided us with an enormous amount of confidence when we spoke. It was easy for us to recall the turmoil through which we had lived. You can do the same with whatever experience you've gained in your life!

So, what's the lesson? Explore your life's experiences and select significant events that have taught you your most valued lessons. You've gained expertise from those lessons. Share the wisdom that you've derived from those experiences and become an expert who speaks.

#16
Be a Reporter Who Speaks

While my former life partner and I were struggling with her mental and emotional illness, I was doing constant research about the illness itself and I became obsessed with the brain and how it functions. I read all I could find about the brain, about depression and how it affects the brain from a medical standpoint, and so much more. I began researching this in the summer of 2004, a few years after she and I got together, and when we had reached the lowest point in our lives.

To this day, I continue to study the brain and how it affects the systems in the body, because I'm fascinated with the way the brain's function relates to every aspect of our lives, including pubic speaking.

Now, when I hold seminars and speaking engagements, I include scientific information that I've researched over the years. Because I've read and studied so much about the brain, I am able to apply this information into my content.

All this reading and researching, in my opinion, doesn't make me an expert on depression or the brain, but it does qualify me as a reporter, as someone who gathers and disseminates that information.

So, with this research in hand, I can add the role of a reporter who speaks to my credentials.

Being an expert is great, and I encourage you to pursue expertise in your area of interest, gaining as much experience as you can. But expertise isn't the only way to qualify as a speaker. Research qualifies you as well.

So, what's the lesson? Research your area of interest as deeply as you can, use that information in your presentations and be a reporter who speaks.

#17
Be a Philosopher Who Speaks

In late summer of 2010, John Heney took the stage at a networking and business education event called "Your Stage," which I facilitate in Ottawa, Canada. Prior to that time, I knew John Heney simply as "John." I knew nothing about John because he was this seemingly nice, quiet guy who came to the events and never said much.

At these events, we invited our members to speak as a regular part of the program, thus the name "Your Stage." On this day, it was John's turn to take the stage.

John's presentation wasn't a retelling of his life experiences, although he did include some of that. His talk wasn't an information session in which he reported on his research, although he included some of that as well. No, the dominant message in John's talk, the gist of his speech, was that we're all on stage all the time, and everything we do is being watched by others, sometimes having an effect that changes their lives. In just a few minutes, John put a new spin on the value of "Your Stage," and personalized its value to each and every person in the room.

John opened our eyes to a new way of looking at the world in which we live. He shared the philosophy by which he lives his life with us, and invited us all to explore that philosophy and see how it might apply to our own lives. He did that by applying his own creativity to a familiar foundation, our event called "Your Stage."

John Heney happens to be a highly educated man. His wisdom and experience are beyond measure and his contribution to the world is vast. He has much expertise and great knowledge and he could have presented himself as an expert or a reporter on any number of topics. Instead, at this session of "Your Stage," John chose to present himself as a philosopher, sharing his insights and creative spin on the world.

What are your philosophies? What personalized and creative spin have you placed on an existing situation? How have you creatively solved a problem in your life? Your creativity and personal philosophies could change the lives of others.

So, what's the lesson? You don't have to be an expert or a reporter to earn the right to speak. Share your creativity and your philosophy and be a philosopher who speaks.

#18
E Is For "Empathy"

When I was twenty-five years old, I was working with a major training organization and was scheduled to speak at a local service club.

When I arrived at the auditorium, I was stunned as I walked into the room and looked around at the audience. The entire audience was comprised of males that looked quite old.

The plan was to have a dinner before I was scheduled to take the stage, so I sat at the head table with my host and some delegates. During the dinner, I asked my host what the average age of the audience members was, and he told me the average age was 84. Now, that wouldn't have been such a big deal if it weren't for the topic I had prepared for my talk: "GOAL SETTING!"

Throughout the dinner, I was trying to come up with ideas for a talk that would be relevant to this group of highly distinguished, profoundly experienced and very old men. I could come up with nothing, so I knew I had to go with my originally prepared plan and speak about goal setting.

After dinner, my host stepped up to the podium and, reading the introduction I had provided him, he brought me to the stage with "…and now, here to speak to us about setting and achieving goals, please welcome Steve Lowell." With those words, and to frail applause, I stepped up to the podium and began by asking, "By a show of hands, how many of you have some clearly defined goals for your life?"

As soon as I finished asking the question, I heard someone in the front row reply, "My goal is to not die before the end of this presentation!"

I've never spoken in a situation with less of a connection to my audience than on that evening. In retrospect, the problem is pretty obvious. I had no idea who my audience was before I got there, therefore, I wasn't able to empathize with them in order to address their interests or stay at their level and pace.

As a speaker, you need to understand the mindset and temperament of your audience in order to speak with them and not at them. This understanding is called empathy, the ability to be conscious of, and have compassion for, the emotional and intellectual state of your audience.

With empathy for your audience, you can tailor your delivery, and sometimes even your content, to resonate with your audience so they can relate to you as a speaker. In return, they empathize with you.

As you're speaking, be aware of the dominant posture of your audience. There's valuable information being shared with you from your audience, and recognizing that information can help guide you into giving the best presentation you can.

In his book, *Winning Body Language*, Mark Bowden describes eight levels of "tension" that really define the different mental, physical and emotional postures we humans can take. The eight levels of tension are: No Tension, Relaxed, Neutral, Deliberate, Alert, Agitated, Entranced and Total Tension.

For our purposes in this book, we need not dissect each level of tension. Suffice it to say that, as a speaker, as you recognize the dominant mental, physical and emotional posture of your audience, you can first match it, in order to gain their trust, and then adjust your tension state as you progress, in order to lead your audience into whatever new state you wish.

Of course, it's impossible to adjust to everyone's individual level, but you can get a feel for the overall mood of the room, and use your discernment to adjust to it. Watch for body language indicators, such as facial expression, nodding or shaking heads, yawning, laughing, leaning forward, slouching, and the crossing of the arms or the checking of cell phones.

These signals help you estimate the dominant posture (tension state) of your audience, and let you adjust your delivery accordingly, in order to form a closer bond.

Recently, I had an early morning speaking engagement with a Chamber of Commerce group near Ottawa, Canada. During the breakfast, before I was scheduled to speak, I tried to get a feel for the dominant posture in the room. I watched the people carefully, spoke to some individually, and also listened to conversations around me, as I tried to get a read on the dominant tension state.

I did this because I knew I was going to be the first speaker, and as the first speaker, part of my job is to make the audience feel like they're glad they came, and also to entice them to stick around for the rest of the morning.

As I began my presentation, I could tell within a very short time that I had misread the group's tension state. My energy level on the stage was too high for them to form that solid bond with me right off the bat. There were no nodding heads, just a lot of blank stares. Most audience members were sitting back in their chairs, some slouching, some with their arms crossed. Many of them were looking straight at me in a semi-catatonic trance.

In reading these signs from my audience, I immediately changed my delivery. I slowed my pace, softened my voice and tempered my movements just a little, all in order to match the dominant posture of the room. I asked a few rhetorical questions to see if I could get some of them nodding their heads, and I made deliberate eye contact with as many people as I could, all the while toning down my gesturing to ensure that my physicality on the stage more closely matched their physicality, giving us the ability to fall in sync with each other from an energy standpoint.

Before long, I could see many of them tilting their heads just slightly showing me an ear, which told me that they we listening. I noticed that many of them moved forward in their seats, and some began taking notes. After a few minutes, I had earned their trust and attention, and I was able to then gradually elevate my energy and bring them with me. This is often referred to as "pacing and leading."

Without that empathy for my audience, I would never have captured their attention and brought them on the journey I wanted to lead them on.

So, what's the lesson? Know who your audience is, and be aware of their feedback so you can match their dominant posture and then lead them to your desired tension state.

Points to Ponder

1. How can you simplify your next presentation?

2. What personal story can you include to enhance your message?

3. What little twist can you add to provide an intermittent incongruity?

4. How can you add confidence to your delivery?

5. What do you need to know about your audience so that you can be empathetic towards them?

6. What role are you taking when you speak? (expert, reporter or philosopher)

7. What experience, research or application of your philosophy will you present to support your role?

CHAPTER 3

TELL A COMPELLING STORY

#19
Decide What Stories to Tell

Think about your life for a moment.

What are your core values? What is the one message you would want to share with this world on your death bed? Who are you, really? What do you stand for? For what or for whom would you fight? What wrongs would you right? What truths would you spread or inequities would you rectify?

Ponder these questions, and come up with your own answers. The answers you come up with will form the basis of your story, the story you will bring to life, and this will help you begin your part in making this world better as a result of your existence.

Once you have an idea as to what your core messages are, even if there is only one, then you can decide which stories to tell to support your message.

What events have transpired that make you who you are today? What people have influenced your character, sense of morality, justice or spirituality? What challenges have you overcome? What adversaries have you claimed victory over? What adversaries have claimed victory over you?

These questions will help you to reflect on your life and to extract events from your memory bank that are worth sharing with the world.

No matter how old you are, or how uneventful you believe your life has been, there are events that have unfolded that make you who you really are. Those are the events you're looking for. Those are the events that can shape the lives of others, because they've shaped your life.

When you share significant events from your life, magic often happens. When someone that has heard your presentation is reflecting on the same questions as you did, their encounter with you becomes a transforming event in their life.

Many of us dismiss our past as boring or insignificant, but that's just not true! Your life is like a string of pearls, consecutive magnificent events that created the person you are today. Explore each one of those pearls and find the magic.

In the spring of 2010, I was reading a post someone had placed on LinkedIn. The post was a comment from someone who had just taken the train from Toronto to Ottawa, a journey of about five hours or so. She noticed that the lady seated directly in front of her did nothing to occupy her time during the entire trip. She didn't read anything and she didn't use a laptop or a blackberry, nor did she listen to music. She had no crossword puzzle or a game of any kind. She just sat and stared out the window for the entire trip.

The person who posted the message simply thought it was weird that anyone could travel for five hours and not have anything to do for the duration of the trip. Her comment was a little judgmental, seeming to express her disapproval of this behavior.

It left me feeling sad that many of us have reached the point where we can't seem to be alone with our own thoughts anymore. We seem to always need some kind of input coursing into our brain in order to pass the time.

When I travel, I rejoice in any alone time I get to sneak in. I get lost in thought; I recall happy memories and hone my creative processes. If I had been on that train, I would have marveled at how this lady just sat there quietly for five hours. Who knows what magnificent ideas and memories were floating around in her brain?

When we constantly pump our brain full of someone else's creative output, we leave no room for our own.

I'm not suggesting that we never listen to music, or read books, or play games. I'm simply suggesting that unless we learn to be still and reflect on life, we stifle our creativity and we miss precious lessons that the events of our life have taught us.

So, what's the lesson? Be still, reflect on the events of your life and find your stories in that silence.

#20
Find the Profundity In the Mundane

We may not realize it, but we gain experience every single day, and if we look closely enough at the events of the day, we can find profundity in many situations and turn that into a lesson worthy of a talk.

About twenty years ago, I was standing in the middle of a river, fly-fishing. I love to fish, and there I was, waist deep in this beautiful river, just having a great, relaxing time when it suddenly began to rain.

I walked over to my day camp along the shoreline, where I had set it up under the bridge where the highway crossed over the river.

It was mid-afternoon and I hadn't eaten anything yet, so I fired up the little grill I brought and began to cook my lunch. I had packed a nice, big, juicy steak, a baked potato, and some veggies.

Now, you're probably wondering why I would bring a steak on a fishing trip. Well, the truth is that I love to fish, but I'm not always successful at it. For this reason, I always bring some food in case I don't catch any fish.

As I was cooking my lunch on the grill, the smoke from the coals began to rise and fill the air under the bridge with the tantalizing aroma of a steak being cooked. The sizzle of the steak, and the warmth from the fire made for an absolutely delightful experience.

It was pouring rain and a little chilly out, but under that bridge, with my soon-to-be-savored lunch, I was toasty warm and very hungry.

As I was getting set to begin enjoying my lunch, I reached out to take my perfect looking steak from the grill, and… SPLAT… bird poop landed on it! A LOT of bird poop!

I looked up to the rafters under the bridge and there were the culprits, two baby pigeons looking over the rim of their nest as if to make sure they had hit their target, and believe me, they had!

The two of them must have fired off at the same time because what landed on my steak was huge! It looked far too big to be from only one of those two little pigeons. Nevertheless, there it was, right smack in the middle of my big, juicy and perfectly grilled steak!

I looked at my steak and considered my options. As it finally dawned on me that my lunch had been destroyed, my bottom lip began to quiver and I felt like the entire day's wonderful feeling was taken away from me.

Many years later, I was invited to be the motivational speaker at the graduation ceremony of a local business college. As I was working out what my message to new graduates should be, to help them as they ventured out into the business world, I was somehow reminded of the pigeon story and created a motivational keynote from it, called "Eagles, Steak and Pigeon Poop." The point of the message was that there are two kinds of people you'll encounter in your life, the ones who want to poop on your steak (the pigeons), and the ones who want to help you soar (the eagles).

My adventure with the pigeons is a simple event, and most of us would forget about it and draw no value from it, but as a speaker, you must learn to explore every event that occurred to you, and find the profundity in it so you can share your stories in a meaningful way with your audience.

I've created keynote speeches from many seemingly mundane events, such as buying a pair of pants, playing a game of darts, and going to a party.

So, what's the lesson? There is profundity in almost every event that you experience. All you have to do is open your mind and your eyes and find the worthwhile lesson in it.

#21
Let Your Story Make Your Point

Here's an example of how a simple story can make a great point.

In 1990, I walked into a clothing store looking for a new pair of pants. I was wearing new sneakers I had just purchased from another store. I was standing by a display of pants when a salesman came up to me and asked, "Can I help you?" I gave the standard response, "No thanks, I'm just looking." He replied, "Well, if you see anything you like, let me know," and off to other business he went.

I selected two pairs of pants that looked identical in every way except for the price. I now found myself needing help. I looked around the store and spotted the salesman who had offered to help. He was standing near the back of the store with another salesman, and I was the only customer in the place.

I caught the salesman's eye and beckoned him over with a wave of my finger. He looked at me with a scowl and held up his finger as if to indicate that I was interrupting him, and I was to wait until he had time for me. Now, had he been helping another customer, I would have understood. Had he smiled and gestured with some measure of friendliness, I would have been satisfied as well. Instead, his posture was completely negative and he was displaying irritation that I would dare bother him while he's in conversation with another salesman. I felt his manner was not appropriate, so I left the store without buying either pair of pants.

I walked into a second store, and while I was looking at a pair of pants, a young sales lady approached me and asked, "Can I help you?" Again, I responded with the obligatory, "No thanks, I'm just looking." She replied, "Well, if you see anything you like, just let me know," and then walked back to the front counter.

I found a pair of pants I liked and tried them on. They fit well and I was ready to make my purchase. I stepped up to the cash register, placed the pants on the counter and pulled out my wallet. Now, in the world of professional sales, we refer to that as a "buying signal."

It seems that our young sales lady went to a different sales school than I did, because she just sat there speaking on the phone and ignored me. Once again, had she been speaking with another customer, I would have understood. But, I don't think it was another customer, because she was arguing with the person about where they were going to have dinner that night.

I waited for a reasonable amount of time, but, since she didn't seem to want to help me any time soon, I put my wallet back in my pocket and walked out of the store.

I walked into a third store. I was standing by a display of pants when another young sales lady walked up to me. I was bracing myself for the usual, "Can I help you?" and was ready to blurt out, "No thanks, I'm just looking."

Instead, her words caught me off guard, because she began with, "My guess is that you're about a size 32, is that about right?" It was about right, so I confirmed it. She continued with, "Are you looking at something for work or for leisure?" and I told her I was playing in a band and that I needed something for the stage. She asked what instrument I played, whether I sit, stand or move around a lot on stage, and about the lights and temperature during the show, and a lot of other questions.

Once I had given her all the answers, she smiled and said, "Come with me." Now, it's a rare occasion that a pretty young lady looks at me, smiles and says, "Come with me," so I eagerly complied!

She walked me over to a display of pants, grabbed a pair off the bottom of the pile and held them out for me.

As I extended my hand and took hold of the pants, she didn't let go of her hold on them right away. Instead, she opened the change room door with her other hand and using her hold on the pants, gently tugged me in the direction of the change room. As I entered the change room she said, "Make sure I see them on you before you make a decision."

I slipped the pants on, and then walked out of the change room so she could see how they fit on me, as she had asked me to do. When I stepped out of the change room, I could see that she had another pair of pants in her right hand, and in her left hand, she held a green shirt on a hanger.

She asked me how the pants fit and I said they were a little snug at the waist. She answered, "I thought they might be. Here, try these on." And she handed me the other pair of pants she had brought. She didn't mention anything about the green shirt she was holding, and I didn't ask about it either. As I entered the change room for the second time, she again instructed me, "Make sure you let me see them on you before you make a final decision."

I tried on the second pair of pants and they fit just great. As she had instructed me, I stepped out of the change room to get her opinion. She looked at the pants, asked me some questions and gave her expert approval. These were the pants I should buy.

Then, a perplexed look came over her face. She looked at me with deep concern and went on with, "You know it would really be a shame."

"What would be a shame?" I asked.

She replied, "It would be a shame for you to be the best dressed guy in the room from the waist down, but to be another one of the crowd from the waist up." And with those words, she stretched out her hand holding that green shirt. Mechanically, I reached out and grasped the shirt as she ushered me back into the change room.

I left that store having spent twice as much as I had intended to, and I was happy about it, all because that young sales professional knew the meaning and value of exceptional customer service.

I included that story here to demonstrate how the simplest of stories can make a powerful point.

So, what's the lesson? Don't just share the lessons found in your stories, share the stories and bring the lessons to life.

#22
The First Ten Seconds Are Critical

When you're telling a story as part of your presentation, you need to set the stage for it in the first ten seconds. Your audience has a very short attention span, and if you begin a story with a long, drawn-out introduction of facts, you'll likely lose them, and then have to work that much harder at getting them back again.

During the first ten seconds of your story, your audience needs to form a picture their minds as to what the situation is. It's not critical that they know how the story fits into your presentation at this point, but they do need to be able to imagine the setting in their minds, so they can follow you throughout your story. As soon as it's clear that you're telling a story, your audience will begin framing the story in their own minds. They need to know who, what, when and where in the first ten seconds. The "why" can be explained later on, that's the suspense factor.

If you move through a story without first painting a picture in your audience members' minds, they'll have a hard time following the events as they unfold, because they'll have no point of reference.

In early 2010, a student in one of my courses spent the first five minutes of her two-minute talk telling us about the history of a little town in England where there was a small shop that sold antiques.

Finally, after the history lesson, she began to tell us about her experience in that particular shop.

Her story was actually very interesting once she got to the heart of it, but for five minutes of what was supposed to be a two-minute talk, she spoke about things that weren't relevant to the event she wanted to share.

I coached her a little, then asked her to tell the story again, so this time, she began this way, "It's twenty years ago, and I'm walking through the doors of a tiny antique shop, in a small town in England."

Can you see how that created a vision in the mind of her audience? By bringing us to a specific time and place and helping us visualize the situation, she captured our attention as an audience, and was then able to take us anywhere she wanted to take us.

So, what's the lesson? Practice the first ten seconds of your story over and over again until you know you have set the stage effectively. Then you can move on, knowing your audience is with you.

#23
Chronology Isn't Important

In my courses we work a lot on storytelling. We do this because there's a greater impact on an audience when they accept a point and frame it into a well-told story. There are many neurological reasons why this happens, but for the purpose of this chapter, suffice it to say that a powerful way to make your point and to have an impact is through your stories.

The most common approach I see in my courses is for a speaker to provide an entire history of the situation, to establish the characters and events before they actually get to the meat of the story.

When you're planning your talk and you're including a story (and I recommend that you do), give some thought to where the story actually begins, and bring the audience to that point right away.

Ask yourself, "When did it happen?" This will help you zero in on the best starting point for your story. Then, flesh in the important details from the event as they're required to round out the story.

Oftentimes, my students will tell me they have information to give that isn't part of the story, but is important to the story, and they think the audience needs to be given all of this information in chronological order. The important thing to remember is that when telling the story, chronology isn't always important. Get right to the point and fill in the blanks as needed.

So far, I've told you at least ten different stories in this book, and if you re-read them, you'll notice that each one begins by stating a year or timeline. Each one answers the question "When did it happen?" This isn't the only correct way to tell a story, but it's an effective way that works. And it makes the story easier to tell.

So, what's the lesson? When telling a story in your presentation, get right to the point of the story. Chronology doesn't matter.

#24
Speaking Is a Transference of Emotion

Why do audiences like stories so much? Because stories help them put the point of the lesson into context, but also add an emotional element to what could be a dry subject.

In addition, our brains are wired to remember emotionally charged events. As we become emotionally involved in a story, our entire being changes at the physical level.

In her book, *Molecules of Emotion*, Candice Pert explains exactly how our emotions physically affect our body, changing the way we behave at the cellular level. Her work shows there are actual physical molecules associated with the emotions we feel, and these molecules bind with receptors on our cells and alter the way our cells behave.

Dr. Bruce Lipton, an internationally celebrated cell biologist, explains in his book, *The Biology of Belief*, precisely how the cells altered by an emotional process affect us at the molecular level. Each molecule has a positive or negative charge, and when they bind with receptor proteins on the walls of our cells, those positive or negative charges cause the proteins in our cells to change their shape, resulting in physical changes in the body.

As a speaker, transferring information only engages the intellect of your audience, but adding an emotionally charged event to your talk brings your audience out of their intellect and into their emotion. That's where real learning is done and that's where real change happens.

So, what's the lesson? Use emotion to help your audience remember you and your point.

#25
Use the Active Voice

When telling your stories, engage your audience's imagination by speaking in the active voice as much as you can. What does that mean? It means making the characters in your story actively involved so your audience can visualize the action.

For example, when I say, "This book was written by Steve Lowell," the first thing you picture in your mind is the book. There is no action. But when I say, "Steve Lowell wrote this book," you picture someone, some representation of me, writing the book. As a speaker, you want to create action pictures in the minds of your audience, and active voice allows you to do that.

There are times, however, when the passive voice is preferable. If the emphasis is placed on something other than a person, or if the person is unknown, passive voice can be used. "The package was sent last week." Notice, however, that there is very little visual context with that statement. Sentences in the active voice have energy and directness, both of which will keep your audience listening.

So, what's the lesson? Speak in the active voice whenever you can. It keeps your conversation livelier.

#26
Get Into Character

Many speakers, especially novice speakers, find it difficult to get into character when they speak. We're so used to speaking in our own, familiar voice and using our natural body movements that stepping outside of the routine makes us feel like we're in some far-away galaxy. We feel self-conscious as our ego kicks in, pulling us back to our own familiar voice and mannerisms.

Your effectiveness as a speaker is directly proportionate to your willingness to let go of your ego, to do what's required to reach your audience. Sometimes, that means doing what others are unwilling to do. Since most people are only comfortable in their own skin, there's a high reluctance to bring forth an alternate character, even for a short time. This means that you, as a speaker, have an opportunity to stand out from the crowd if you can step outside the confines of your own ego and bring your story to life by getting into character.

If the character in your story is angry, show your audience what anger looks like. If your character is sad, show your audience what sadness looks like. Learn to step into the moment and animate your characters while you speak, and your audience will love you for it!

So, what's the lesson? When telling stories, the more you can get into character, the more powerful and interesting your story will be to your audience.

#27
Speak In the Present Tense

Writing in the past tense can create a very compelling story. As speakers, many of us can tell a story in the past tense and still make it compelling, but if you want to stand out as a speaker, you'll need to engage the audience better than other speakers do, and an effective way to do this is by telling your stories in the present tense.

In the summer of 2009, a very sweet lady named Penny Lee attended an evening workshop I was giving on public speaking and networking.

One of her assignments was to come prepared to speak for two minutes about a significant incident in her life.

Her speech began something like this, "Three years ago, I was working with the 'Party Light' gift company. I was really successful and sold enough of the products to earn an award of ten-thousand dollars. At the ceremony, they called me up onto the stage to accept my award, and I was very emotional because I realized that I was finally able to buy my husband the motorcycle he always wanted."

At this point, I asked her to start her story over again, but to make two changes to it. First, I asked her if she would tell the story in the present tense, and second, I asked her to begin the story as if she was hearing someone call for her to come up to the stage.

This is roughly how her story was told the second time, "The time is three years ago, and I'm sitting in a huge crowd at a national convention for the 'Party Light' gift company. I hear my name being announced over the microphone and I'm called to the stage. I walk onto the stage and notice a sea of faces watching me as the host hands me an envelope with my name on it.

I open the envelope and it contains a check for ten thousand dollars! I was just awarded this check as a bonus for my sales performance.

I hold the check in my hands, and I'm feeling very proud, because I can finally buy my husband that motorcycle he has always wanted but could never afford."

Penny Lee then broke into tears of pride and joy right there in front of the class. As she did, a hush came over the entire room and I could see other students holding back their tears.

So, what's the lesson? By taking her story and telling it in the present tense, Penny Lee was able to turn it into a magical experience for her audience.

Points to Ponder

1. What events have transpired in the last month which might make a compelling story?

2. What lesson can you extract from those events?

3. How will you grab your audience's attention in the first ten seconds?

4. What emotions do you want your audience to experience as you tell your story?

5. What characters need to be brought to life during your story?

CHAPTER 4

PREPARING TO MASTER THE STAGE

#28
Know Why You're There In the First Place

Here's an important idea about your speaking objective: have one!

It was the spring of 2010 and I was sitting in a large conference room, listening to one of the keynote speakers.

The speaker stepped on the stage and took us back to her childhood, recounting sexual abuse. From there, she moved into her teen years when she had difficulty making friends and had an issue with drugs. As she confided in us, we, as an audience, began to sympathize. I was quite impressed that she had the courage to stand before us and share these very personal stories and I was curious to hear where she was going with all of it.

As she continued recounting the difficult periods of her life, her drug addiction, her time in rehab, a failed marriage and financial ruin, you could sense the audience was getting weary of the never-ending flow of grief coming from the stage. I knew we were all good and ready for this talk to move on to the victorious ending that brought it all together in a happy-ever-after conclusion.

After speaking for twenty minutes about her grueling misery, her personal testimonial got to her bankruptcy and that was how she ended her talk. There was no happy ending. There was no evident ending at all. There was no point, no lesson, and no advice in her speech. There was nothing! It was like a movie that just stops in the middle without resolving anything.

Unfortunately, this person had been through more than anyone should have to endure, and she most likely had tremendous wisdom that she derived from all those challenges. How many lessons were in there that she didn't share with her audience?

I do feel compassion for this woman and all she's been through. I still honor her courage to share her trials with the world, and I'm sure that her motives were positive. It's just unfortunate that she would go through all that and leave her audience with absolutely no lesson of value.

When you speak, know what you're there to accomplish and prepare your talk, your speech or your presentation in order to accomplish your goal.

So, what's the lesson? When you speak, have a goal. Know why you're there.

#29
Start With the Goal and Work Backwards

In the previous point, we discussed the importance of having an objective for your presentation. Even though the objective is reached at the end of the presentation, it should be the first thing you think of. Your entire presentation will be designed to get to that objective.

What are some possible objectives to a speech or presentation? Are you there to inform, inspire or influence? What do you want your audience to do, to be or to have as a result of your presentation? How will you let them know your intention, and how will you get them to take action?

Once you have clearly defined your goal, a logical next step is to prepare your closing. How you close your presentation or speech will determine what your audience does with the information you've provided.

Prepare your closing statement, or your "call to action," and then consider what your audience needs to know and feel in order for them to take the course of action you recommend. Most audiences are going to require more than personal influence to make changes, to make decisions or to take action, therefore, your presentation must contain compelling arguments to sway them to your way of thinking.

After your goal is clearly defined, and you've worked out your call to action, then it's time to decide what content will best convince your audience to adopt your ideas.

Designing your presentation from the end first is a good way to make sure you include only the relevant information in your presentation, because at each point you can ask yourself, "Does this point help me reach my goal?" It's difficult to answer that question if you don't know what the goal is.

So, what's the lesson? Start from the end and work backward to make sure your presentation supports your goal.

#30
Use Sticky Notes to Help You Prepare

Here's a little trick I learned years ago that helps when preparing a talk or presentation. Get a pack of three-inch by three-inch sticky notes, then find a large, open space such as a door or a wall with no pictures on it.

On the first sticky note, write the objective of your talk or presentation and stick it on the wall or door in the top left corner. This will become a reference point for building the rest of the presentation.

Next, on separate sticky notes, write any idea that comes to mind about your presentation topic, without judgment as to its value or relevance to the objective. Jot down any ideas, stories, examples, anecdotes, research, references and anything else that come to mind about the presentation. For each thought, place the sticky note on the wall, in whatever order you feel it should be placed.

When you're done, you should have a space filled with sticky notes, each with one thought written on it. Then walk away from it for twenty-four hours.

After twenty-four hours, come back to the space and review the material on the sticky notes. Look for anything that doesn't feel right or look right and place a small "x" on that note, so you can identify it later as something needing attention. Mark it with a question mark if you're not sure yet. Maybe something needs to be reworded or relocated somewhere else in the presentation. As you're reviewing, new ideas may come to mind, so add them to the presentation wall.

Repeat this for a few days, always adding and moving things around. Try not to remove too much just yet, but if there are things that are not likely to fit into your presentation, move them to another spot, maybe on another wall. Don't discard them. We'll discuss why a little later.

After you've completed this review several times, and when you're confident that you have all the points you need on the wall, then it's time to begin removing items. The next section will explain how and why.

So, what's the lesson? Use sticky notes to gather your creative ideas in one place, and add to it every twenty-four hours. You'll be amazed at how much information you can come up with.

#31
For Every Point, Ask,
"Is This Really Important?"

After another twenty-four hours, come back to the space and for each sticky note on the wall, ask yourself this: "Is this point really important? Is it absolutely critical to my presentation?"

If the answer is 'yes,' leave the sticky note on the wall. If the answer is 'no,' remove the sticky note, but keep it handy for later. I like to place them on a separate wall, because I'll be coming back to them.

Once you've passed first judgment on all the thoughts and added any new thoughts, walk away for another twelve to twenty-four hours. Can you see why it can take so long to prepare a really great presentation? This is the difference between a good presentation and a kick-ass presentation!

Keep coming back to the wall every twelve to twenty-four hours or so, until you have only the most critical thoughts on the presentation wall, all arranged in the order in which you will present them.

Now, it's time to begin adding the supporting information.

Go back to the pile of sticky notes you removed from the wall and sift through them for information that supports your main points.

When you find sticky notes with information you can use, post them into your presentation, and in the proper location. Your presentation will take shape, and when you're through, you'll have everything you need on the presentation wall. You may need to come back to the presentation wall every twelve to twenty-four hours or so for several days until you have it just the way you want it. That's just what it takes to do this well.

In his book, *Beyond Bullet Points*, Cliff Atkinson provides a presentation template that breaks the presentation down into triads. This means there are three main points. For each point, there are three supporting points, and for each supporting point, there are three additional supporting points.

When the presentation is arranged in this way, you have three versions of the presentation. If you have five minutes to present, you can deliver only the first three points, if you have fifteen minutes to present, you can deliver the first three points and each of the supporting points. And if you have forty-five minutes, you can deliver all of the supporting points in the presentation.

The benefits of preparing a presentation using this sticky note approach are numerous.

You'll have a well-organized presentation that's been thought through carefully and strategically.

You'll be able to deliver variations of the presentation, based on the amount of time you're allocated. Since you have five-minute, fifteen-minute, and forty-five-minute versions of your presentation, you'll be able to adjust your delivery on the fly if circumstances warrant.

This process also galvanizes the information in your brain, so you're far more likely to be able to flow through the presentation without referring to your notes.

You'll have a pile of extra sticky notes, each with information that could be added to your presentation if needed. This gives you enormous confidence, because you have a lot of extra material if you're asked questions, if you're given extra time or if your presentation flows faster than planned. Many of those extra sticky notes probably contain great fillers to add to your presentation if you have to.

So, what's the lesson? Plan your presentation with sticky notes. They'll help you trim it down and keep it relevant.

#32
Memorize Key Phrases
But Not the Entire Presentation

Relying on your memory for your entire presentation will really get you into trouble. That's why most speakers use notes and/or slides to help them stay on track, which is okay, as long as they're not just standing there and reading to the audience.

Keeping that in mind, it's a good idea to memorize and rehearse key phrases and sentences, so they have the desired impact when you utter them.

When I give a presentation of any kind, I always write out the opening statement. I research the best way to say it, and rehearse it over and over again. When I take the stage, the first thing that comes out of my mouth is something I've said thousands of times before. This way, I get off to a comfortable start, and I gain momentum right from the first word.

The same principle applies with my call to action and my closing statement. These are critically important parts of the presentation, so I memorize them, rehearse them and refine them to the point that they roll off my tongue with ease, with confidence and with impact.

When developing your presentation, identify the critical points and make sure you know how you're going to deliver them. Come up with the best way to articulate your thoughts, and practice it relentlessly. Your presentation will have the impact you need, but still have the natural flow your audience wants.

So, what's the lesson? Memorize and rehearse key words and phrases, and they'll have the impact you require. Leave the rest to a natural delivery.

#33
There's Power In Three

There's significance to the number three when speaking. The concept of providing information in blocks of three is known as the "tri-colon," and is a secret that's been used for ages in literature. The theory is that it's simpler and more efficient for the brain to absorb and apply meaning if there are three words or ideas, instead of two. A third word in a series not only gives confirmation and completes a point; it's the earliest stage in a phrase at which the connection between the first two words can be supported. When you use more than three, your audience members' brains begin to pay less attention to the information. When you use fewer than three, your point falls short of its intended impact.

The "tri-colon" is a staple of effective writing and speechmaking, and the world is replete with examples of powerful "tri-colons" that have shaped our culture. Chances are pretty good that you're familiar with, and know the meaning of, these famous "tri-colons."

- The truth, the whole truth and nothing but the truth
- Father, Son, and Holy Spirit
- The Good, the Bad, and the Ugly
- Life, liberty, and the pursuit of happiness
- Stop, drop, and roll
- Location, location, location

So, what's the lesson? When planning your presentation, arrange your points so they're in groups of three as much as possible.

#34
Remember the Ten to Twelve Rule

According to John Medina in his book, *Brain Rules*, you have ten to twelve minutes to hold your audience's attention, and then they start to drift away from you. If the information in your presentation isn't too boring but not overly exciting, you'll need to build something that breaks the flow of information every ten to twelve minutes.

Studies reviewed by Dr. Medina confirm his findings on this matter. It seems that before the fifteen-minute mark of a normal presentation, the audience has checked out. There's no real consensus as to precisely why this occurs, but it's been substantiated. So, what does that mean to you?

It means that, when you prepare your talk or presentation and it's going to be longer than ten to twelve minutes, you'll want to include something to snap your audience out of their mental pattern and reengage their attention. So, how do you do that? Try telling a story, offering an example or showing an exhibit or demonstration—anything that gets your audience's mind out of their intellect, and into their emotions or creativity.

The key here is to make sure the material included to break the flow of information is material relevant to the subject at hand. Use the opportunity to further enhance the learning experience, as opposed to redirecting the audience's attention completely off topic.

So, what's the lesson? Plan to interrupt the flow of information every ten to twelve minutes.

#35
Present A "Holy Sh*t!" Moment

In his book, *The Presentation Secrets of Steve Jobs*, Carmine Gallo explains that every presentation given by Steve Jobs, business magnate and co-founder of Apple, has what he calls, a "holy sh*t" moment. This is a moment in the presentation where Jobs presents something so awe-inspiring that the audience is stunned.

An example of a Steve Jobs "holy sh*t" moment is when he pulled a laptop computer out of a plain manila envelope. The crowd was stunned.

As you may recall, back in Chapter Two, at point twelve, Julia pulled her wig off while she was on the stage, now, that was a "holy sh*t" moment. Or at point thirteen, also in Chapter Two, when Katrina slipped on her lawyer's robe and gave this catchphrase, "When the gown goes on, the gloves come off," that was a "holy sh*t" moment.

In a presentation I gave to my business education and networking group called "Your Stage," I created a "holy sh*t" moment by showing a bar graph of the average membership fees of local business groups. To demonstrate how our own membership fees compare, beside that bar on the graph, I revealed an animated bar that grew far higher than the competitor's fees and then suddenly dropped to about half. That moment garnered some gasps and a ton of new memberships.

One of our guest speakers at the event began his presentation with, "Several years ago, I spent $135,000 on a dog!" Now that was a "holy sh*t" moment! He then went on to explain he'd always wanted a dog, and his wife agreed that if he bought a specific house that she wanted, he could buy the dog, so he bought both.

How important is it to include such a moment? Well, few presentations actually have one, but the memorable presentations usually do. Look for opportunities in your presentation to wow your audience with something that will give them a moment of pause. If there's no such opportunity, so be it, but if you can find one, there's gold in that opportunity.

When creating your presentation, think about what you can do that's out of the ordinary, that's different from what anyone else has done. Think creatively and let your imagination soar. Of course, it's important to confine your "holy sh*t" moment to what's proper and acceptable. Stay away from anything controversial, or anything that could be offensive to audience members, unless offending them is your goal.

So, what's the lesson? See if you can find a "holy sh*t" moment in your presentation. Your audience will remember you!

#36
Avoid Jargon-Creep

Keep your language simple and universal whenever possible. Unless you're speaking to a closed audience made up entirely of industry members who understand the buzz words, stay away from acronyms and slang.

Computer people are especially prone to this. (I can say that because I'm one of them!) We like to use cool acronyms and techno speak because we know how to do that. Secretly, at least for us guys, it's because we think that if we use all the coolest words and jargon, all the pretty women will want to have sex with us. So far, that theory hasn't proven to be as solid as I originally thought!

Nevertheless, the urge to impress your audience with huge words and acronyms that only the cool people know can be pretty powerful. For the benefit of your audience, who only wants to be impressed by your message, open up your language to the masses and use wording that everyone in the room can understand.

I once watched a spiritual speaker who gave a thirty-minute talk, and apparently, it was about the use of our spiritual nature to manifest our desires. For thirty minutes, I listened to huge words and spiritual jargon that made zero sense to me. To this day, I still have no clue what he was talking about. I just didn't get it at all.

So, what's the lesson? Keep the language relevant to the audience. When in doubt, simpler is better.

Points to Ponder

1. What exactly is your objective for this presentation?

2. What do you want your audience to do, be or have as a result of your presentation?

3. What are the key points of your presentation? (answer this only after you have completed the process using sticky notes)

4. How will you break the flow of information every ten to twelve minutes?

5. What will be your "Holy Sh*t" moment?

6. What jargon might you be using that could potentially alienate some of your audience members, and what words could you use instead?

CHAPTER 5

PREPARING YOUR MIND FOR STAGE MASTERY

#37
Don't Worry About Being Perfect

For my entire life, I've been a musician. I've played in bands since I was very young and have traveled the country performing live on stage and recording in studios. My best friend, Dave, was always with me in these bands. We've always played music together.

In the late 1980s, our band broke up, so Dave and I decided we were going to do things differently. We decided we weren't going to find another drummer and bass player. Instead, we were going to enter the age of electronic music.

We went out and purchased all the latest electronic equipment and hibernated for a year in the basement. We learned and programmed the drums, the bass and the background orchestration so he and I could be the only ones on the stage. With Dave at his keyboard, and me playing my guitar, we could present a full band sound with only two guys.

After a year of programming and rehearsing, we took to the stage and for the next ten years we performed as a duo. So, what does all of this have to do with public speaking? Read on, and you'll see.

As we played, we could always feel a difference between the music from the computer and the music that used to come from our live band. The difference was that the music coming from the computer was perfect. It was flawlessly timed and it was perfectly in sync, with any dynamics that existed being deliberately programmed and based on instruction, not on emotion. There was no human appeal to the music that came from the computer.

Fortunately, as Dave and I performed, we were able to add the human touch for the audience, by being imperfect. But the background music, though authentic in sound, was mechanical in feel, because it was perfect.

As a speaker, perfection could give your speech a mechanical feel in the eyes of your audience. Certainly, too may "ums", or "uhs" and other such "word whiskers" will dilute the impact of your talk. A good thing to remember is, unless you're competing in a formal speech competition, imperfections are not only tolerated by your audience, they're expected and welcomed because they make you more human.

Be aware of excessive distractions in your delivery, but there's also no need to stress over putting on a perfect performance. Let your talk flow naturally, and let your emphasis change as you reach your emotional connection to your message.

So, what's the lesson? Enjoy yourself when you speak, without worrying about perfection. Just be human, and let the message guide you.

#38
Your Self-Talk Matters

There's an old axiom, often attributed to Dr. Joyce Brothers, that states, "You can't consistently act in a manner which is inconsistent with the way you see yourself."

The way you see yourself is directly affected by how you talk to, and about yourself. Any personal-development guru will tell you that. Therefore, as a speaker, you'll want to replace any self-talk that doesn't serve your message and image with self-talk that does.

This isn't just a motivational tool. Your self-talk leads to physical changes in the way you behave, in the way you speak and in the way others perceive you. When you speak well of yourself, or even when you repeat positive and accepting words in your mind, your physical posture actually changes. You stand straighter, you become more animated with your gestures and you just feel better all round. Try it, and see for yourself.

Marc Bowden, author of *Winning Body Language*, calls this your "Yes State." When you focus on all the most positive words you can think of, several great things happen. Not only do you become more open and accepting toward yourself, but you also become more open and accepting toward your audience. They'll feel that openness and acceptance from you. They'll trust you more when you're in this state, because the open and accepting posture and energy will provide them with an unconscious feeling of being accepted by you. That's a good thing!

If you don't see yourself the way you'd like to see yourself, the objective is to make sure your self-talk is always positive and empowering. Since you can't consistently act in a manner which is inconsistent with the way you see yourself, how you see yourself is largely determined by your self-talk, therefore, make your self-talk reflective of how you'd like to see yourself. Get it? Your speaking will be greatly enhanced by a strong and healthy self-image. You'll feel it, and so will your audience.

So, what's the lesson? Positive self-talk only, please!

#39
Acknowledge Your Stage Fright, Then Go on

We covered the truths about stage fright in Chapter One, but it's worth revisiting, because it's such an integral part of presenting that we need to know how to deal with it when it arises.

When we were performing, sometimes we'd play a really important show and I'd get stage fright in a huge way. Even though I was highly experienced and prepared, I sometimes worked myself up into a frantic state by projecting the worst-case scenario we've spoken about. I couldn't play properly because my hands shook so much, my mouth got dry, my voice shook and my brain turned itself off. Fight or flight syndrome to the max!

My strategy back then was to try and talk myself out of the anxiety, to convince myself that all the bad things I projected in my mind would never happen. The main reason this never worked is because all the bad things I projected in my mind usually did happen! I'd break guitar strings at the worst possible times. My guitar would cut out when I was in the middle of a great solo. My microphone would begin to crackle, lights would burn out, patch chords would simply break, and my guitar strap would unhook itself. I mean, everything that could possibly go wrong always seemed to go wrong for me at the worst possible time, always and for years!

After a while, I learned to accept the fact that I was going to have to deal with all these crazy things happening to me. They became part of the show. When I finally accepted these things as part of my reality, the anxiety seemed to fade away. Funny thing is, after a while, so did the crazy things!

It's possible, and more than likely, that crazy things kept happening as they had always done, that perhaps I'd made such a big deal out of them when they did happen before that I was making them out to be bigger than they actually were. The point is that when I accepted the fact that performing also means dealing with crazy things, the anxiety subsided and turned into positive, fun energy. The same thing happens when speaking.

Crazy things are going to happen when you speak. Accept them as part of the show. Your hands may shake, your mouth may get dry, your voice may crack and your stomach may feel sick. It all happens, so acknowledge these things when they happen. Accept them as part of the speaking process. Eventually, they begin to become less of a problem and, sometimes, more of an asset. But chances are excellent that they'll never go away entirely.

So, what's the lesson? Stage fright exists. Accept it, acknowledge it, and make it part of your show.

#40
Apply the Switching Strategies

In her ground-breaking book, *Your Destiny Switch*, *New York Times* best selling author, Peggy McColl shares fifteen simple and profoundly effective strategies for switching your emotional state from negative to positive. When I read this book for the first time, I remember thinking how relevant her insights are to speaking and performing.

Since speaking is mostly transference of feeling, it's important that you feel the right emotions when you speak, in order to keep your emotional state congruent with your message.

To apply the fifteen strategies effectively, McColl suggests that you first acknowledge your emotional state, and observe how you're being affected, both physically and mentally. Then, you need to make a clear decision to change your emotional state if needed. If you decide you need a change, you move on to the first step in deploying the switching strategies.

The fifteen strategies are:

Slow your breathing.

Get away, even if it's just into another room for a while.

Nature meditation. Go outside and stare at a flower or a tree for one minute or so.

Mini meditation. Take a few moments alone to detach yourself from your thoughts.

Use Humor. Humor releases endorphins that help lift your mood.

"Snap" out of it. Wear a rubber band around your wrist and snap it to remind yourself to apply these strategies.

Create a Verbal Cue. A few words can act as the rubber band to remind you to make the conscious decision to feel differently.

Get Moving. Physical activity increases oxygen to your brain and clarifies your thinking.

Attend to your body. The benefits of a healthy body are obvious.

Listen to positive music. Music triggers emotions in your brain. Listen to the theme song from "Rocky" and see how it affects you.

Connect with positive people.

Use your imagination. Create an imaginary experience and trigger positive emotions. Take a luxury car for a test drive or try on an expensive suit.

Use your memory. Think about a time in your life when you felt emotionally elated.

Reach out and help someone else.

Replace negative thoughts with positive thoughts.

Your Destiny Switch, by Peggy McColl is a definite "must read" for anyone in the business of speaking or performing.

So, what's the lesson? Follow the above fifteen switching strategies, to switch from a negative emotional state to a positive one.

#41
Take a Leap of Faith

The reason you're the one on stage is because you have something to say, right? But often, our ego jumps in the way, and we begin thinking more about whether people like us, rather than whether our message is getting across the way we want. Unfortunately, when we're preoccupied with our ego, we can't possibly perform as well as we otherwise could, and our message suffers.

As speakers, we need to take our egos out of the equation while we're in front of an audience, and we need to lose ourselves in our message in order to take the audience on the journey we intend for them to take. So, how do we do that?

Sometimes, it takes a leap of faith. Faith that when you let yourself go, and let yourself get absorbed in your message, the audience will also get absorbed in your message, and be positively affected by it. There's no real way to know how well your audience will receive you, but you can be certain that the deeper you immerse yourself into your message, the more your message will be felt by your audience. The important thing is to keep your focus on the benefit to your audience, not on your own personal gain. When you direct your mental focus on yourself, your audience will feel it, but when you direct your mental focus on presenting something of value to your audience, they'll feel that too.

Of course, there are extremes. A popular video on 'YouTube' shows Phil Davison, a Minerva, Ohio, councilman, giving a crazy speech in an effort to gain the Republican nomination for Stark County treasurer. Now, this guy got lost in his message! Yes, it's great to get lost in your message, but you also need to balance it with some degree of good judgment. There's a difference between having a sincere emotional involvement in your message, and simply going on a rant.

So, what's the lesson? Sometimes you need to take a leap of faith. Make it about your audience, not about you.

#42
Who Should You Emulate?

My speaking hero is Zig Ziglar.

When I was first learning to speak formally, I had this great idea that, if I could just emulate Zig, I could be a great speaker too. So, I began studying his talks, learning some of them word for word. I practiced his mannerisms and his jokes, and I began to speak like a Zig Ziglar clone.

Imagine my surprise when people didn't respond as well as I thought they would when they expected a Steve Lowell presentation, and got a Zig Ziglar impersonation instead. And a poor impersonation, at that! I even attempted to mimic Zig's southern drawl from time to time, and I believe it didn't go over very well, since it was exacerbated by the fact that I'm Canadian, eh! I'd be at some meeting in the Great White North, speaking like I was fresh off the train from Yazoo City, Mississippi!

It wasn't long before I realized the world wasn't interested in me being a Zig Ziglar impersonator. Now, an Elvis impersonator, maybe, but alas, I realized I needed a new persona.

That's when I discovered Tony Robbins. Now, here's a guy I could imitate! He's cool, people like him and he has no drawl. I thought, "*I can do that!*" So, my new persona came out as Tony Robbins on steroids. When I spoke, I'd blast onto the stage at warp speed, puff out my puny little chest to make myself look huge, and then I'd whoop and holler as I bounced around the stage, screeching about goal setting and self-image. All this time, I had a lousy self-image and no clear goals for myself. Then, one day it hit me. Who was I trying to kid? The more I tried to be like the successful speakers, the less successful I got.

I spent some time working on my own self-image, trying to discover who I really was, and what I really stood for. I struggled with all the rules I was being taught about speaking, because none of it felt natural, none of it felt right to me. When I became an instructor with a major training organization, I was pressured to follow the rules they laid out as to how I presented myself. The way I spoke, the words I used, the way I stood. I was being molded into a genetic clone of all the other trainers employed by this world-wide company, and I complied. My new persona became that of a robot, mechanically programmed to comply with the company's procedures for speaking and training.

After a while, I began asking myself, "Why? Why do I have to stand like that? Why do I have to use those words and not my own? Why can't I just be myself when I'm speaking or instructing?" I became fed up with the pressure to conform, the pressure to follow someone else's rules because they said I had to, and I decided to move on to something better.

At this point in time, I discovered something that changed my life forever. I discovered who I am and what I stand for. I believe our responsibility is to use our freedom of expression to present ourselves authentically, and let our experiences enhance the lives of others.

Notice that I said "responsibility" and not "right." The reason I view our authentic self-expression as a responsibility lies in the fact that I believe we've all been given the gift of taking a journey through life, not only to evolve our selves, but also to contribute positively to the growth and evolution of others. If we gather the lessons and wisdom gained from our lives, but don't share those lessons and that wisdom through our words and our expressions, no one else will have benefited from our journey.

So, when questioned about who you should emulate, the answer is no one. Yes, you may select a few specific traits or mannerisms from your heroes, and mold them into an effective delivery to enhance your own style from time-to-time, but, above all else, be yourself.

So, what's the lesson? Be yourself. Everyone else is taken.

#43
Become A Better Listener Of Life

It's amazing what you can learn, just by listening more! What should you listen for? Everything and anything! Most of us get so caught up in our own daily lives and our problems that we spend most of our mental time solving those problems. We're worrying, strategizing and creating an image in our minds of that worst-case scenario that we spoke about in chapter one. Unfortunately, this pattern makes us oblivious to all the sensory input that's around us, and there's great value in that sensory input!

One of my favorite musicians is the new-age sensation, Yanni. Now, Yanni tells a great story about an occasion when he was in Venice, Italy, and he was just sitting there, listening to the sound of a nightingale that was perched on his window sill.

The nightingale has a very distinct voice, a voice that's very sweet and reaches high into the musical registers. Yanni explained that many years later, he came across a musical instrument called the Chinese flute. When he heard the sound of this instrument, it reminded him of the song of the nightingale. He then wrote a magnificent piece of music, using the Chinese flute as the focal instrument in the song of the nightingale. If you've never heard Yanni's performance of "Nightingale" live, go to YouTube right now and look it up. You're guaranteed a captivating and emotionally uplifting experience.

Again, you might ask what this has to do with speaking. Once again, the answer is, "Everything!" The world around you is filled with sounds that can inspire you, sounds that can move you or uplift you, that can balance you or anger you, and more. Listen to nature, listen to people, and listen to the sounds of the city and of the country. Take your headphones out of your ears and just listen to life! When you learn to listen to life, you'll find more inspiration than you'll ever find in your iPod.

So, what's the lesson? Listen to life, and draw your inspiration from what's already all around you every single day.

#44
Pay Attention to the Person in the Mirror

Before speaking or performing, I always pause a minute or so, and I take a good look at the person in the mirror. I do this for several reasons:

I want to visualize who my audience is going to be seeing. This helps me to put myself in their shoes a little, and it elevates my understanding of what their experience will be like. It's all part of having empathy for my audience, as I mentioned in the SPICE section of chapter two.

I check to make sure that I'm physically prepared to present, that I don't have to worry when I walk out onto the stage. I check to make sure that my tie is properly tied, and whether there are obvious imperfections of which I'm not aware, such as a green thing between my teeth.

I give myself a little pep-talk. A mini "Rah! Rah!" session to help elevate my belief that I will do the best I can do when I take the stage in a few minutes.

The last thing I do is to give myself a mini pat on the back. A personal "Atta-boy" for pursuing my passion, and getting myself to this spot, on this day, and being ready to do my work.

So, what's the lesson? Give yourself a little personal encouragement and accolades for a job well done, before you begin to speak. It will lift your confidence, and elevate your empathy for the audience.

#45
Rehearse Everywhere, All the Time

In late 2009, I gave a ten-minute presentation, about presentation skills, to a networking group. Afterwards, someone asked me how much time one should use to prepare for a presentation. My answer was simply that there's no set amount of time someone needs to prepare. Presenters need to prepare until they're as ready as they can possibly be. Essentially, no amount of preparation is too much.

Later, I calculated how much time I spent preparing for that ten-minute presentation, and the answer was almost fifty hours! That doesn't mean I sat at my computer preparing slides, researching material, and working on the presentation for fifty hours. Preparation includes rehearsal as well, and not all rehearsal happens on a stage.

To be ready for that ten-minute presentation, I prepared the information, created the slides, gathered my evidence, and then rehearsed. I practiced how I was going to open and how I was going to close the presentation, out loud and in my head. I worked out the questions I'd ask the audience, and even to whom I would ask some of them. I visualized the entire ten-minute presentation in my mind over and over again. I rehearsed it in my mind while I was in the car or in the shower, and even while doing house work. Whenever I could afford the mental time to do so, I rehearsed the talk.

I approach every talk I give the same way. I run it through my mind thousands of times. I stand in front of the mirror and run through sections of my talks. I set up a video camera and record myself rehearsing the talk in my basement, and then I review those videos. I try out my talks on my wife, and then I get her feedback.

Now, here's an important point. You're not rehearsing in order to memorize the talk word for word. You're rehearsing so you can deliver key phrases the way you want them to sound. You're rehearsing so you can remember the order of your points and familiarize yourself with your material so well that you won't have to rely on notes.

So, what's the lesson? When you have a talk to give, rehearse it all the time, everywhere you can, in your mind and out loud. Rehearse it until you know your material so well you could talk about it in your sleep.

Points to Ponder

1. What new self-talk will you use leading up to your next presentation?

2. How does stage fright manifest itself in you?

3. What switching strategies will you use to maintain a healthy mindset?

4. Who are your favorite speakers and which of their characteristics might improve your own delivery?

5. When will you rehearse your presentation?

CHAPTER 6

Preparing for a Powerful Delivery

#46
Use PowerPoint Sparingly

When I was preparing for the ten-minute talk I mentioned throughout the last point, I created a deck of slides and spent several hours getting them just the way I wanted them.

Each time I rehearsed my talk, I either ran the slides through in my head or had them projected on a wall while I rehearsed. During the entire preparation process, I felt there was something not quite right about my presentation, but I couldn't really put my finger on what it was.

I felt completely prepared for my talk, but there was still something bothering me, even as I sat in the car on the way to the event. I asked myself several mental questions, including, "Have I missed any important points?" "Does the presentation flow the way I want it to?" "Is everything in the best possible order?" and, "Are my PowerPoint slides properly prepared?" The answer to all of these questions was "yes," so what was bothering me?

Then, a question popped into my head that I had not yet asked myself, "Do I really need those PowerPoint slides at all?"

I considered that for a moment and visualized how the presentation would flow without the slides, and a weight was lifted from my mind. That was it! I didn't really need those slides to accomplish my objectives for this presentation. I delivered the presentation with no slides, and it went as beautifully as it could have gone. PowerPoint slides wouldn't have helped my presentation, and most likely would have hindered it.

One might think it was a waste of time preparing those slides. Not at all, the preparation time on the slides helped me galvanize the material in my mind, even though I didn't use those slides. I knew my material so well, I didn't need those slides to help me present it, but I did need them to help me prepare.

Something similar happened in the summer of 2010 when I was preparing a mission-critical presentation for my members at "Your Stage," my business education and networking group. I was preparing for a one-hour sales presentation to increase membership and I'd prepared 140 PowerPoint slides.

I set up the projector, and rehearsed my presentation hundreds of times, changing slides and reordering things as I went along. I spent hundreds of hours on those slides and in rehearsal and preparation.

Two days before the presentation, I went through every slide and asked myself, "Is this slide critical to the presentation?" If the slide was not absolutely pivotal in making the point I was trying to make, I deleted it from the deck. I narrowed 140 slides down to 10 critical ones. 10 slides that were absolutely mandatory to make my point the way I needed it to be made. The end result was that I knew my material so well I didn't even need to look at the slides when they came on the screen, and I was free to adlib if the mood struck me, or if I felt I had to change course for my audience's sake.

The presentation went exactly as I'd envisioned it, and my mission was accomplished with only ten awesome slides.

PowerPoint slides can be a powerful addition to your presentation, but they also bind you to a specific order of events, limiting your freedom to take the presentation into a new direction if you choose, or if required.

So, what's the lesson? When preparing your next presentation, ask yourself this question, "Is this slide critical to the presentation?"

If the slide isn't critical, remove it. PowerPoint slides are meant to enhance your presentation, don't let them detract from it.

#47
Avoid Bullet Points Like the Plague

In his book, *Beyond Bullet Points*, Cliff Atkinson provides the best explanation I've ever read as to why bullet points can kill your presentation. He explains that when an audience is watching a presentation, there are two basic tracks of information going into their brain. There's a visual track, and there's an audio track. To maximize the impact of the information for the audience, both tracks should be used.

You'd think using bullet points makes sense then, because when you're speaking and you've got a slide with bullet points on it, you're providing both the audio track (your speaking) and the visual track (your slides). But there's a problem with that conclusion. When your audience is reading words, they're not using the visual track; they're using the audio track.

That sounds very strange. How can they be using the audio track when they're reading the words? Because, when we humans read words, our brain translates those words into sounds so we can place them into the context of language. This means that as you're delivering your speech, your audience is reading the words on the slides at the same time, and since both the verbal words and the written words are using the same audio track, then the visual track isn't being used.

Furthermore, our brain doesn't process verbal words and written words at the same speed. When reading words, the neural processing is much slower, because our brain has to translate those words into sound. Verbal input doesn't have to be translated. So, we end up with two flows of information coming through the audio track at different speeds. This dilutes the learning process for your audience.

The net result is that your audience is trying to both listen to your words and to read your bullet points, which means the impact of both is reduced.

So, what's the lesson? Avoid the use of bullet points if at all possible.

#48
Use More Pictures and Less Text

The pictorial superiority effect, or PSE, is a phenomenon caused by the fact that text and pictures are handled differently by the human brain.

Text is seen as a collection of tiny pictures, and the meaning of each letter has to be assessed and put into context with the adjoining letters in order to make a word, which requires neural functioning and some time. Pictures, on the other hand, require far less neural processing and have the added advantage of more easily engaging the emotions.

A series of tests referred to by John Medina in his book, *Brain Rules*, show that people could remember more than 2,500 pictures with at least 90 percent accuracy after several days post-exposure, even though they were exposed to the pictures for only about ten seconds. A year later, the accuracy rates had only dropped to around 63 percent.

According to Medina, if a presentation is delivered orally, your audience will remember about 10 percent of the information after seventy-two hours. If you add a picture, the retention level increases to 65 percent.

Pictures don't just dress up your presentation; they directly, and significantly, affect the measure of learning and information retention enjoyed by your audience.

So, what's the lesson? Use more pictures and less text in your presentations.

#49
Please Don't Ever Do This...

Bob is a real estate lawyer, and a member of the same group as Katrina and me (from item number 13 in Chapter Two).

A few weeks after Katrina's presentation, it was Bob's turn to present.

Bob chose to use PowerPoint slides for his presentation, and on each slide were bullet points supporting his talk.

In addition to bullet points, Bob included a small cartoon on every slide. These cartoons were very amusing, and everyone laughed at each one. We were all very interested to see what clever and funny cartoon Bob had on his next slide.

Bob went through his presentation, and he managed to keep his focus on his material, never once commenting or referencing the cartoons on his slides, much like the way Katrina never commented or referenced the garment bag on the table until the end of her presentation. It was really an interesting process to watch Bob remain focused on his material, while the rest of us laughed at the cartoons on his slides.

Everyone highly enjoyed Bob's presentation, and when it was over, we all gave him tremendous words of praise and congratulated him on his entertaining approach. We did this quite sincerely, because Bob's presentation was truly entertaining and enjoyable.

A few days after Bob's presentation, I ran into someone else who had been part of Bob's audience. She commented on how much she had enjoyed Bob's presentation, and she said, "I particularly liked the cartoon about the cat."

I responded, "Yes, that was funny! Let me ask you this, do you recall what Bob was talking about during that slide?"

She had no clue, nor, in fact, did I! To this day, I can't recall one single point that Bob made in his presentation. I have no idea what Bob's presentation was about, and I can't recall a single message.

Bob's presentation was entertaining, and maybe that was his purpose. But as an audience member in that presentation, I still know nothing more about Bob's business than I did before he presented. In my judgment, even though all the information was there, that presentation did not fulfill its purpose.

In Chapter Two, we explored the concept of intermittent incongruity. This would be a good time to gauge if that concept was applied correctly by Bob.

Bob used a PowerPoint presentation in the traditional manner, filling page after page with bullet points. The difference was that he added a cartoon on each slide. Why did he do this? Was it because he felt his information might not have been interesting enough to hold our attention? Or maybe he felt that we, as an audience, just wouldn't care about his information. So, he likely added the cartoons to provide some entertainment value and something of interest.

After Bob's first few slides, my brain spotted a number of patterns:

- When Bob changed the slide, a new set of bullet points appeared.
- Each slide contained a cartoon.
- There was no correlation between the cartoons and the information on the slides.
- Each cartoon was funny.
- Each slide was boring.

John Medina explains that the brain will not pay attention to boring things. In addition, he states that the more attention the brain pays to a given stimulus, the more that information will be retained. So, how does this apply to Bob's presentation?

The bullet points on the slides were boring, so my brain paid no attention to them. The cartoons were funny, so my brain did pay attention to them. In the end, no attention was paid to the information in the presentation, because all the attention was paid to the cartoons. All I remember are the cartoons, and only one or two of those.

Bob may have been hoping that adding the cartoons (incongruities) would create interest in the information. In actual fact, the opposite happened. The bullet points were boring, but the cartoons were interesting, so the incongruity between the information and the cartoons caused an attention diversion from the presentation to the cartoons. And since the cartoons never proved to be relevant to the information, no attention was ever paid to the information, only the cartoons.

So, what's the lesson? Don't put anything in your presentation that's going to distract your audience, unless it's relevant to the presentation.

#50
Provide Evidence

Regardless of how you present yourself, either as an expert, as a reporter or as a philosopher (see Chapter Two), you'll need to provide some evidence that you have actually earned the right to be in front of your audience. Inevitably, you'll have someone in your audience who'll be asking the question, "Who says so, besides you?" or, "Why should I believe you?" Having the proper evidence gives you the ability to handle any such questions, and you may very well have to use this evidence.

When you have the proper evidence to support your talk, you remove yourself from any line of fire of anyone who might challenge you. This provides you with enormous confidence, because you know that you have the goods to defend yourself against someone who might oppose you. You have all the proof you need, and that gives you strength.

In addition, providing evidence helps your audience to put your information into its proper context in their minds. It allows your audience to see the real-life application of your ideas, your claims or your philosophy.

The evidence you provide can depend on how you position yourself when you speak. If you're presenting yourself as an expert, your evidence is your personal experience. As a reporter, your evidence is your research. And as a philosopher, you offer an example of the application of your philosophy.

When my wife, Jayne and I speak about our experiences in business together, we share many stories with our audience. We give true accounts of our experiences that support the purpose of our talk. As long as our accounts are factual, no one can challenge the validity of what we're saying, because our evidence is our experience. In addition, when we share our own experiences, our audience can reflect upon the similarities and differences between our experience and their own, applying our information to both. This allows them to visualize how our information might apply personally to them.

When I speak about my former partner's illness from a scientific standpoint, I present a lot of data and information that I researched. I present myself as a reporter. My evidence is the information I've researched and the sources from which it came. I'll have copies of the books that I reference, and I'll hold the books high in the air for all to see when I reference them. This way, if someone challenges my information, all I have to do is refer them to the book. If they want to challenge the book, so be it, but that takes me out of the line of fire.

Disclosing my sources also allows my audience to obtain their own copies, and to follow their own research, if they so choose. As a reporter, your evidence is the research you've done and the sources from which that research came.

In Chapter Two, I mentioned John Heney, who was a guest speaker at my business education and networking event called "Your Stage." In John Heney's presentation at "Your Stage," he shared some of his philosophies with us. In his presentation, he also shared his personal accounts of how he applied his philosophies to heal himself from an illness that cripples almost everyone it touches. At the end of John's presentation, he not only shared his philosophies, but he also provided examples of their application.

As a philosopher, your evidence is in the examples of how of your creative spin was applied to resolve a problem.

So, what's the lesson? Providing evidence to support every point you make boosts your confidence, enhances your credibility, and helps your audience apply your information. Always have an answer for the questions, "Who says so, besides you?" and, "Why should I believe you?"

#51
Get the Facts

Statements beginning with, "Studies show..." or, "Experts believe..." and, "They say..." are not examples of good evidence.

If you're going to present a claim, and then state that it's supported by studies, by experts or by others, you should know which studies are being referred to, what experts you're talking about, and who "they" are. You should also know the actual facts and figures, whenever possible.

Television commercials are notorious for providing vague evidence to support a claim. For example, a commercial might refer to studies claiming that seven out of ten dentists recommend a specific brand of toothpaste. You've probably seen those commercials. In reality, how much faith do you place in those claims? How well does the evidence really support the claim?

If the commercial referred to a 2010 study, completed by the American Dental Association, in which 10,000 dentists were surveyed, and 7,000 of those dentists recommended ABC toothpaste over all other brands, would you find that a little more credible? Most people would, and so would a live audience.

When presenting results from studies, relevant statistics or cited quotes as evidence, it's always a good policy to identify the source, and even have a copy of the actual report, of the book or the article in your hands, held up nice and high as a visual cue when you refer to it.

In my keynotes, I'll often refer to scientific information. When I do that, I refer to a recognized expert, provide the expert's name, and the title of the book, then, I'll raise the book up for the audience to see. This way, my audience knows that I have facts to back up my claims, and there's an actual source they can see.

Providing specifics whenever possible lets your audience know that you've actually done your homework, and it prepares you to answer the question, "Who says so, besides you?"

So, what's the lesson? When providing evidence, provide specific facts and sources as much as possible.

#52
Answer the Tough Questions Before They're Asked

Always plan for a question and answer session, even if you never do them. At some point, your host is likely to address the audience with, "Are there any questions for our speaker?"

You need to be prepared for this eventuality. Before you speak, think about your content and consider what questions might come from it. Develop your answers well in advance, so you're armed with the information, should it be required. In addition, carry any supporting evidence you might need to substantiate your answer. It's very impressive when an audience member asks a question, and the speaker is already prepared with an answer, complete with evidence.

On the other hand, you may hold a question and answer session, and have no questions asked. This can be highly uncomfortable for a speaker. So, what do you do?

Having a list of questions handy can get you out of this jam in a flash. If you open the floor to questions and there are none, this doesn't necessarily mean that there aren't any questions. It more likely means that no one's brave enough to ask one. So, wait a few seconds, and, if it becomes apparent that there are no questions about to be asked, simply take control by saying, "One question that's often asked is…" State a question and then answer it. This technique will not only take the pressure off you, by eliminating the awkward silence, but it may also prime your audience to open up and pose additional questions.

So, what's the lesson? Always have answers for the tough questions in case you need them.

#53
Be Prepared To Go Off Course

It's bound to happen, especially in a business presentation. You'll be in the middle of your presentation and someone will interrupt with a question or a comment that derails your entire plan. What to do?

This is an extension of the previous point. If you're presenting to an audience who's likely to be interactive, to pose questions, and to make comments throughout your presentation, you'll need to be prepared to handle it with grace and poise.

When preparing your presentation, consider all the angles. Look for possible openings where someone might interject, and be prepared with whatever information that may be required to handle it. You might even consider preparing slides and visuals, and have them ready just in case.

When speaking to a larger audience, it's less likely that you'll be run off the road, but in a smaller presentation with a group of decision makers, it's not only possible, it's likely, so be prepared.

If you have every angle covered before you enter the presentation room, your confidence will be elevated, and your delivery will reflect that.

So, what's the lesson? Be prepared to be derailed.

#54
Remember To Repeat

In Chapter Four, we explored the process of building your presentation from the end. Begin with the goal and work your way backward. During your talk or presentation, repeat key points that lead your audience toward your goal.

If your intention is for your audience to take action as a result of your presentation, you'll need them to retain some information from your presentation for a while after you've finished speaking. In order for them to do that, the information must enter their long-term memory. To get into long-term memory, it first has to pass through working memory (formerly known as short-term memory). Unfortunately, information can only reside in working memory for about ten seconds, and then it's gone.

The brain is always scouring the sensory environment for new input, looking for patterns and trying to predict what's going to happen next. Because of this, whatever information finds its way into working memory is quickly replaced by new information.

In 1885, Hermann Ebbinghaus discovered the exponential nature of the brain's ability to forget data. His research shows that the speed in which the brain forgets depends on a number of factors, such as the difficulty of the learned material, how the material is represented and such physiological factors as stress and sleep deprivation. His research also shows that one way to galvanize information into long-term memory is through intermittent repetition.

While Ebbinghaus' studies relate mostly to measuring memory over the course of months or years, the principles hold true on more micro levels as well, such as minutes or days.

So, what's the lesson? Spaced repetition is like glue that helps information stick in the mind of your audience. Select the primary message of your presentation, and repeat it from time-to-time, to help your audience retain the message and be able to take action when you've completed your presentation.

Points to Ponder

1. Read through your slides for your next presentation. Which, if any, are 100% critical to making your point? Delete the rest!

2. For each bullet point on your slides, What visual representation that might be more effective?

3. Review your entire presentation. Is there anything in there that might distract your audience to the point where they are no longer listening to you? If so, remove it.

4. What facts or claims are you making in your presentation, and what evidence do you have to support them?

5. What are the tough questions that your audience might ask and what will be your answers?

6. What opportunities are there in your presentation to be taking off course and how will you handle them if they come up?

CHAPTER 7

Arriving at the Gig

#55
Be Early

One of the worst feelings in the world is rushing to prepare to take the stage.

If I'm speaking somewhere within a reasonable driving distance, I'll leave early enough that I can arrive at my gig at least an hour early, and usually earlier than that. It's important to find the location and get comfortable once there, so that I can go through my pre-gig rituals, discussed in the rest of this chapter, as well as in chapter eight.

Leaving early also allows me to take my time when driving, so my mind is free to rehearse my presentation at a comfortable pace, knowing that I have loads of time to get where I'm going. That rehearsal time is of tremendous value in helping me confirm in my own mind that I'm as prepared as I can be.

When I have to fly somewhere, or when it's a longer drive, I avoid traveling on the day of the event. I'll travel the day before I'm scheduled to present. The primary reason is the likelihood of delays. At the time of this writing, I have never missed an engagement due to travel delays, all because of this policy of mine.

The other reason I prefer to travel the day before an event has to do with physical energy. Even a comfortable train ride, a short flight or a leisurely drive can be tiring, and I like to conserve my energy for the stage. I recommend that you consider following the same policy, whenever practical. When you give yourself enough time to relax, to run through your mind exercises, and to properly prepare yourself for show time, it reflects well on you as you deliver on the stage.

So, what's the lesson? Arrive early, and give yourself time to prepare mentally and emotionally.

#56
Check the Equipment

Checking the equipment may sound like an obvious thing to do, but I've often seen presenters arrive at an event, only to find out their laptop doesn't work with the projector, or the presentation is in the wrong format for the computer, even though the presenter has supplied everything.

If you're bringing your own presentation equipment, such as a laptop and a projector, for example, always check that everything's in working order before you leave for the gig. Check everything! Set up your projector and hook the laptop to it, and then run through your delivery either the night before, or the day of, your presentation, to double check that everything you need will work.

Sometimes, however, this just isn't as simple as it sounds. In the winter of 2010, I arrived at a location to do a sales presentation for a corporate client and they had a specific room fully equipped for these types of presentations. They had all the latest gadgetry, including a smart board, some wireless microphones, and a high-end projector, to name a few items.

I had requested, and expected, a computer with a very specific software package installed on it, in order for me to do this presentation, and I was assured the computer would be ready. When I arrived, I checked with the IT guy to confirm that the software had been installed, and he assured me that everything was ready.

I arrived about 90 minutes early, so I fired up the projector, the microphone, the smart board, and the computer to test everything.

As it turned out, the software I needed was not installed, even though I'd been told it was. I tracked down the IT person, and it took him about 45 minutes to find the software and get it installed, thankfully, well before my presentation began. The result of being early was that the delay was seamless to the audience. Had I not checked the equipment, my presentation would have started out with a 45-minute break, while the software was being installed.

Although it wasn't my fault the software wasn't installed, I was responsible to ensure that everything was ready for my presentation.

So, what's the lesson? Test everything you can before you speak. It could save your presentation.

#57
Get To Know the AV Person

If there's a person in charge of the equipment, such as the sound and the lighting, make sure to find out who that person is, and introduce yourself. Generally, the person who does the sound, the lighting and the projection is one of the least recognized people on the team. I know, because I've been that person myself.

When you find out who the AV person is, and you acknowledge them, get to know them a little, and offer your appreciation for their work. They tend to value that and will likely remember you, because not many people extend them this courtesy.

This may not garner you any special privileges or a better sound, but the AV person may be a little more aware when it's your turn to speak, and may be a little more attentive, simply because you got to know them a bit and they want you to succeed up on the stage in front of an audience.

In addition, if you do need a little extra help, such as a specific lighting effect or a louder monitor, they're more likely to help you out if you've been sincerely appreciative of their work.

It's a minor point that could make a difference to your overall experience.

So, what's the lesson? A little sincere appreciation for the AV person could enhance your experience as a speaker.

#58
Have A Plan B for Everything

I don't use PowerPoint very often, but I will if it enhances the material I'm about to deliver. I also prepare another version of the same presentation, only this one doesn't require the visuals. I do this in case I arrive at a location to speak, and the projector that was promised doesn't show up, or it doesn't work for whatever reason, yet, I can still go on with the presentation.

In early 2010, I was making my first presentation to my Business Education and Networking event called "Your Stage." I was presenting an education piece on why bullet points shouldn't be used in a presentation. I'd spent many hours creating an animated slide deck that visually demonstrated how information flows into the brain. My slides were well designed, but complex in their animation, because the complexity was required in order to demonstrate the process properly.

As I began explaining the process, my computer went black. For no obvious reason, it just shut itself off. The timing couldn't have been more precise. It was as if Murphy himself was standing by with a remote control, and timed the blackout with expert precision.

I simply kept speaking, as if the computer switched off at my command. Instead of using the slides to provide a visual of the process I was explaining, I described it using gestures. I'd already practiced this in advance, just in case I needed to go to a plan B, and it turned out that I did have to. I had a plan B, and I always have a plan B, because things go wrong fairly regularly.

Being prepared means more than just knowing what you're going to speak about, it means that you're prepared for every conceivable contingency. Prepare for the best, plan for the worst, and deliver what's required.

So, what's the lesson? Consider everything that could go wrong, and have a plan B, because you'll need it at some point. It's a near certainty.

#59
Look At the Room

Being told to, "Look at the room" might sound ridiculously simple, but there's a good explanation for this. One thing that can throw a speaker off their game immediately is the shock of looking into a sea of faces looking back at them from the audience. The room has a different view from the stage, and it can be highly intimidating.

One way to minimize this stage shock is to walk up to the front area of the room, even if it's off the stage, and peer into the room to get a feel for what the vista looks like. Even if the room is empty at the time, examine the area the audience will soon be occupying, so you can familiarize yourself with anything that might cause a distraction.

In the fall of 2010, I was hired to conduct a workshop for an accounting firm. One of the owners of the firm is also a martial arts instructor, and he'd purchased the neighboring office space to create a dojo for the staff to train in, as an extracurricular perk. They also use the dojo as a training room, where they hold workshops and seminars. When I arrived to do my workshop, the seats had been arranged in a fashion that left me facing a long wall that was essentially a huge mirror. Because I arrived early, I stood at the front of the room and considered whether or not I'd be distracted by the mirrored wall. I decided I should be facing the other way, so I rearranged the entire room. Now, I was facing the back wall and the audience was facing the mirrored wall. I felt the risk of having some of the audience members distracted by the mirror was a lesser evil than having me distracted by the mirror. I was being paid for my services. The client deserved my very best.

So, what's the lesson? Get a visual of the room in advance, that way there are no surprises when you take the stage.

#60
Feel the Room

Have you ever noticed how all rooms have their own feel?

There's a facility in Ottawa where I hold many events. This facility holds three conference rooms. The room we'll use for our event depends on the expected number of guests, since the rooms are in three different sizes. Not only are they different in size, but each has a unique look and feel.

One of the rooms is small and very bright. It's beautifully decorated, with paintings on the walls, a huge skylight, and large windows at one end. The second room is the largest, also nicely decorated, but not quite as elegant as the small room. The third room is mid-sized. This room's dimly lit, the ceiling tiles are stained, and the carpet's red. It's a very dark room.

I've spoken in all three of these rooms on many occasions, and the experience is unique in each room. When I watch videotapes of my presentations, I notice there are very subtle differences in how I present from one room to the next. For example, in the small room, which is bright and elegant, I tend to be smoother, because I feel more polished speaking is such an elegant room. I'm more intimate with my audience, because it would typically be a smaller audience and I'm physically closer to them.

In the large room, there's less intimacy, and I feel more like a performer, because I'm delivering my presentation on a larger stage. I seem to be a little more animated and lively when speaking in that room.

In the darker room, I seem to have a little less energy. The dimmer environment, the older carpets, and the stained ceiling tiles give the room a tired feel, which ultimately affects its occupants. Having noticed this on video, I deliberately pick my energy up a notch when I'm speaking in that room, in order to compensate.

What does all this mean? It means that the feel of a room can affect how you present, in subtle but important ways. If you're aware of these subtle differences, "feeling" the room can help you make minor adjustments, in order to give your best performance.

So, what's the lesson? Be aware of the feel of the room, and your response to it, so you can give the audience your very best.

#61
Listen To the Stage

Just as one room feels different from another, the sound also carries differently.

The sound in a room can be affected by countless factors, including the type of carpet on the floor, the height of the ceiling, the existence and the location of windows. There's nothing you can do about most of those things, but there's one thing you should be aware of that offers you a small amount of control. It's something few speakers pay attention to, and maybe that's the reason I've never read or heard of anyone else making this point, but you should listen to the stage itself.

Many facilities will have a portable stage that can be taken down and moved at any time. The potential issue with these types of platforms is that they're typically hollow, and, if cheaply made, will make booming noises when you walk on them.

We became particularly concerned about this type of staging when we were playing in the band, because a hollow stage often meant a thunderous echo would reverberate from the floor as we pounded on the drums, or danced around on stage. Now, as a speaker, it's not likely that you'll be quite that dramatic. Although, if you like to walk around the stage like I do, there can be a disruptive effect.

Hollow stage platforms often resonate when you walk on them, and your microphone can pick up that sound and amplify it, booming through the room. Because the tone of that sound is very low, it can be like a bass note roaring across the audience, and it's terribly distracting.

I've seen many speakers who were clearly unaware of the thunderous boom from the hollow stage as they stomped across it, because, often times, the person on the stage can't hear it. You'll want to either test it yourself, if you have access to the empty room, or pay close attention to the previous speaker and see if they're generating the booming effect as they walk around on stage. If the effect is happening, you'll know that you need to tread lightly on your feet, in order to avoid creating the same distraction.

So, what's the lesson? Listen to the stage to see if it generates a hollow, booming sound when you walk across it.

#62
Scan the Stage or Platform

I recently gave a presentation to a government department, in a room that was built like a theater. It had rising seats, a large, low stage at the front, and a raised podium on one side of the stage. Behind the stage was a huge screen. The screen went from ceiling to floor, and was as wide as the stage.

This configuration had major implications for me. I was using PowerPoint slides in this particular presentation, and my slides were critical to the message. This particular government department keeps heavy security; therefore, I was required to send them my presentation ahead of time. They loaded it up on their own system, so I was at the mercy of their stage configuration. The challenge for me was my lack of ability to travel across the stage, as is my regular rhythm, because I had to remain behind the podium, otherwise I'd obstruct the screen.

In addition, the podium was equipped with a wired microphone, and a mouse for advancing the slides. Both the microphone and mouse cable were only long enough the reach the podium; there was no room for wandering.

Having taken a good look at the stage area well ahead of my presentation, I was able to foresee the restrictions, and to adjust my delivery accordingly. Had I not taken the time to become familiar with the stage area, I might have inadvertently tried to pull the microphone onto the stage, or disconnected the mouse from the presentation computer, or walked right out in front of the presentation screen, any of which could have presented an awkward moment. I would've been able to easily recover from any of these little distractions had they occurred, but avoiding them by being aware just made me appear that much more professional and prepared.

So, what's the lesson? Look for anything on the stage or platform that might restrict your normal delivery, so you can make any required adjustments, in order to avoid awkward mishaps.

#63
Find Someone Friendly and Speak With Them

In early 2011, *New York Times* best selling author, Peggy McColl, spoke at my business education and networking group called "Your Stage." The first thing she did when she took the stage was to ask everyone in the audience to smile. She said she doesn't really like speaking in public, and the smiling faces help to calm her down. Of course, the entire audience gave her a nice big smile. Our official photographer, Ima Ortega, snapped some great pictures, and Peggy went on with an amazing presentation.

Was it all just a nice act? Not at all, there's tremendous value in knowing that you have allies in the audience, especially if you're a novice speaker. A good way to secure a few allies is to make a few new friends before you go on the stage. I do that by scoping out the room and hand-picking a few people who seem friendly. I then approach them, and make a friendly connection, have a little chat and get to know a little about them. There are two benefits to doing this.

The first benefit is that knowing someone in the audience, even a new acquaintance, gives you a feeling of comfort. It's a psychological anchor you can use to emotionally ground yourself if you're feeling anxious.

The other benefit is more practical in nature. It gives you something familiar to refer to when you're speaking. I even like to mention my new contact, especially if they're someone prominent in the group. Let me share an example.

I was speaking at a large networking function in early 2010, and I didn't know anyone at this function. Not a soul. During the opening segment of the meeting, there was an opportunity to mingle, so I made a few connections. I conversed with a few attendees for a while, and picked up some information that was pertinent to my talk. When the time came and I began my talk, I mentioned my new contacts by name, and referenced some pertinent parts of my conversation with them. "I was speaking with Bill Dobbs before the session this morning, and we discussed the fact that most people don't have an agenda when they attend a networking function." All of a sudden, anyone who knew Bill Dobbs felt a tiny bit of a connection with me as well, because I mentioned someone familiar to them in the conversation. Another benefit was the fact that Bill felt like a hero, because he'd had a personal impact on the presentation. It was a win-win situation for everyone.

So, what's the lesson? If you don't know anyone in the room, find a friendly face and make a new connection.

Points to Ponder

1. Remember to arrive early so that you can check all the equipment and get to know the AV person if there is one.

2. What could go wrong and what is your "plan B"?

3. Remember to look at and get a feel for the room, stage and audience.

CHAPTER 8

Just Before Show Time

#64
Review Your Notes

I'm frequently asked if I ever use notes on the podium when I speak. The answer is that I do, in a manner of speaking.

On occasion, I'll have notes on paper, but very rarely. If I do have paper notes, they typically hold only keywords, not a script. If I'm in the role of Master of Ceremonies, I'll have notes with the order of events, but, generally, my notes are in the form of pictures in my head.

I'll create a visual stack of pictures in my mind that serves as a road map for my presentation. As I speak, I review the pictures in my mind, and that helps keep me on the right track.

I do, however, always review my notes, whether they're on paper or in my head, a few minutes before I speak. This is to make sure I have a recent exposure to the material so my recall is better. The purpose is not to memorize the speech, but to refresh the key points in my mind.

Some people run into difficulty here, because they try to do a last-minute run through of their entire speech or presentation, and then get frustrated when they can't remember the entire thing. That frustration leads to anxiety, which reduces the ability of the brain to focus. The presentation is doomed before it begins.

By being properly prepared, all you'll need is a list of keywords to help you recall the order of events. Review this list before you go on, not to remember the content, but to remember the order.

So, what's the lesson? A last minute review of the order of events will help you stay on track.

#65
Rehearse Your Opening Line

Even an experienced speaker may, on occasion, forget his or her opening words.

I was speaking at a "Your Stage" event in early 2010, and there were many people in the audience who were attending the event for the first time. Many of these first-timers were there specifically to hear me speak. I had a great presentation prepared, and I was excited about the opportunity to present to this group.

Since this was my own event, I was responsible for the set-up before the event began. When I arrived, I was busy setting up the screen, then the projector, and finally the laptop, on top of taking care of many little details that go along with hosting a presentation. In addition, I had to meet, to greet and to mingle with my guests.

Because of this, I didn't get the quiet time I need to refresh my thoughts before I speak, therefore, I didn't rehearse my opening line. Though I had it prepared, and had rehearsed it many times before this day, it wasn't fresh in my mind because of all the distractions before the session.

When the time for me to speak came up, the Master of Ceremonies introduced me as I stepped onto the stage. I suddenly found myself with nothing to say. I looked into the faces of the audience, and my opening line completely escaped me. In silence, I tried to reach into my memory banks to find the words, but there were none to be found.

After what seemed like a month, I finally found some other words to open my presentation with, and I recovered quickly after that.

I built up some momentum, and the presentation went smoothly onward. It was, however, an awful feeling when I found myself at a loss for words, even though it was for a few moments only. I was nearly overwhelmed, and the longer the words escaped me, the more the level of anxiety rose. Of course, as professionals, we're expected to make it completely transparent to the audience, and I believe I was able to do so in this case, but it could have gone the other way. Had I not been able to generate some other opening remark in reasonably short order, my confidence would've gone south in a hurry and my presentation along with it.

So, what's the lesson? Always rehearse your opening line a few minutes before you take the stage.

#66
Take Some Quiet Time

In the summer of 2004, I had the good fortune of spending a weekend with John Assaraf, author of *The Street Kid's Guide to Having it All*, and *The Answer*. John is also a teacher, based on his world wide book phenomenon, *The Secret*. During our time together, John taught me about universal laws, and the power of the human brain. This is where my research into the brain's function began.

One of the most impactful things John taught me that weekend was the incredible power of meditation.

After teaching us the mechanics of meditation, and how to clear our minds of thought, he let us practice for a while so we could build some skill level at it. He then gave us each a spoon. He led us through a short meditation, and before we knew it, we were bending spoons with our hands. I don't mean making little bends in the handle of the spoon; I mean tying the spoon in knots, like it was a string, and all this with zero effort! The moment I applied conscious thought to what I was doing, the moment I started thinking, "Hey, I'm bending a spoon!" the bending stopped, and the spoon became a solid object again.

John explained that the unconscious mind can be accessed through meditation, opening the doors to powers that are blocked by the limitations of our conscious beliefs. In addition, it has enormous rejuvenation benefits.

There is research to support John's teachings. In 2007, scientists at the Flinders Medical Centre, working in the Centre for Neuroscience branch, completed the first scientific demonstration of the changes in brain activity when a subject is in a distinct meditative state. Their research confirmed the benefits of meditation on alertness, among other interesting results.

So, what's the lesson? As a speaker, any mental advantage you can acquire is of value, and a short meditation session before you speak can boost your alertness and energy significantly.

#67
Stretch Your Face

I've done some research on how many facial muscles one uses when speaking. I have yet to really find an answer that can substantiated with facts. According to Wikipedia, there are nineteen facial muscles. How many of them do we use when we speak? Who knows? But I do know we definitely use a few.

To help you articulate your words more comfortably and more smoothly, it helps to stretch your face muscles.

First, find a location where no one can see you, because if people see you doing this, they may have you taken away in a little white jacket, with a drool cup hanging around your neck! Now, open your mouth as wide as you can until it hurts a little all around your mouth. Stretch it for about five seconds, to loosen up the skin and muscles surrounding your mouth.

After those few seconds, repeatedly say, "Why," with a huge exaggeration of the mouth. Begin with your lips tightly pursed, and open as wide as you can while saying, "Why." Do these stretches seven to ten times, and open your mouth as wide as you can on each occasion.

Once done, it's time to reverse the motion. Begin as wide as you can, and say, "Yow," closing your lips in a tight purse. Repeat this step seven to ten times as well.

Then, over-pronounce each vowel three or four times, stretching your face and tongue on each vowel. This will stretch all of the muscles you use to speak, and loosen the skin around your mouth so the words flow easier as you deliver your speech.

I have to give you a few words of caution about this process. Perform this stretching about fifteen minutes before you speak, and any red marks caused by the stretching have time to disappear before you take the stage.

So, what's the lesson? Stretch your face for more fluid pronunciation.

#68
Loosen Up Your Voice

You know that singers do it, right? You should do it too. Even if you can't sing a note, you should loosen up your vocal chords before you speak. It's very simple. Just take some time alone in your car, in your hotel room or outside somewhere, and practice singing the, "do-re-mi" scale.

Why should you do this? Because speaking is just like singing, when you speak, you don't maintain a constant pitch, volume, pace or tone. Your voice varies in order to apply emphasis as you speak. When your vocal chords are exercised, they loosen up and are free to express a variety of pitches and tones.

But there's also a benefit that's a little less obvious. Your vocal chords also help control your breathing, because they can close up and stop air from passing through.

When we get nervous, our muscles tense up. Our vocal chords are muscles, so they tense up as well, not only making speech more difficult, but making breathing more difficult.

All I do is my "do-re-mi" scale a few times in different pitches and at different volumes. I don't force anything, or push my voice hard; I just apply a normal amount of volume and effort to get the vocal chords in motion. This helps me breathe, and helps my words flow more fluidly.

So, what's the lesson? Loosen up those vocal chords before you speak, and you'll breathe easier as well as speak better.

#69
Get Your Body Moving

There's a very simple concept around that implies exercise improves your brain function.

When blood courses through your brain, it doesn't just distribute nutrients, it also carries oxygen molecules that act like sponges to soak up the waste products, and transport them out of the brain. The more oxygen sponges you put through there, the cleaner and more efficient the brain will be.

When you exercise, you increase the rate of blood flow across the tissues of your body, by stimulating your blood vessels to manufacture a flow-regulating molecule called nitric oxide. Exercise helps to create new blood vessels that further enhance the distribution of blood to the body tissues. The more blood vessels you have, the more those oxygen sponges can clean up.

The same thing happens in your brain. Imaging studies have shown that as you exercise, there's an increase in blood flow to a region called the dentate gyrus, which works with the hippocampus, a region directly associated with memory.

In addition, blood flow to the brain enhances the growth of something called Brain Derived Neurotrophic Factor (BDNF), a sort of fertilizer for your brain. BDNF helps keep your neurons young, and helps your brain form new ones.

So, what's the lesson? Movement in the body increases blood flow to the brain, which makes you smarter!

#70
Adjust Your Mental and Physical Posture

In a recent public speaking workshop I conducted, I had the entire class, consisting of about fifty people, stand up and look straight ahead. I asked the students to take note of exactly what they were seeing at eye level. Next, I asked them to close their eyes, and to think about the words they were about to hear as I recited them. I began uttering a string of positive words and phrases, such as, "Yes I can, amazing, tremendous, and absolutely." I kept this up for a minute, and then told them to open their eyes, and to take note of exactly what they were seeing at eye level now. Finally, I asked them to raise their hand if what they were seeing now was at a higher fixed point than what they were seeing before they closed their eyes, and 100% of the hands went up. I've repeated this exercise several times since, with the same results.

What does this tell us? It tells us the positive words improve not only your mental posture, but also your physical posture.

Clearly, if you are about to take the stage, you want to be in the most productive mental and physical posture you can. Shortly before you speak, take a few minutes and run a series of positive, empowering words through your mind to help elevate your mental and physical posture. You don't even have to close your eyes; you can do this on the fly.

As you perform this exercise, you'll feel your emotional state lift, and you'll notice you're seeing things that are at a higher fixed point, and that you're standing a little taller. All these things enhance your performance as a speaker.

So, what's the lesson? Adjust your mental and physical posture with positive words, and your entire attitude and physicality are enhanced.

#71
Don't Rely on Them to Tell You

Many years ago, I was teaching at 'Willis College of Business and Technology' in Ottawa. I was sitting on the front corner of the teacher's desk, explaining a point to the class, and I could feel something amiss about the energy level in the room. The class, comprised mostly of women, seemed to be in a strange, an almost silly, mood.

I concluded that it was due to my magnetic personality, causing the class full of women to be so capricious in my presence. Then, one of the ladies at the back of the room held up her hand. I acknowledged her, and she said, "We have a problem."

"What's the problem?" I asked.

"Your fly is down!" She replied, as she giggled. I looked down, and saw that she was telling the truth. Not only was my zipper down, but, because of the manner in which I was sitting on the edge of the desk, there was also a gaping hole to make it easier for the class to peer into my pants. I looked completely ridiculous!

Before I entered the class room that day, I had chatted with at least a half dozen other people, any one of whom could have drawn my attention to the open crater in my midsection. However, it was my own responsibility to check those things before I stepped up to teach, and I neglected to do so.

When I was in high school, we had one geography teacher who always wiped the chalk off the board with his hands. (Back then it was chalk boards, not white boards.) He would then unconsciously wipe his hands on the seat of his pants.

Every time he turned his back to the class to write something on the board, there were two giant hand prints on his butt. As far as I know, no one ever mentioned it to him, because we all thought it was too funny. Maybe he did it on purpose, who knows? But the point is that none of us were going to tell him how foolish he looked.

Before you speak, go into the bathroom and examine yourself in the mirror. Make sure your zipper's up, your suit pockets are empty, your hair is the way you want it, your tie is straight, your dress or skirt isn't clinging, and you're happy with the way you look. Most importantly, make sure there aren't any green or black things stuck in your teeth!

So, what's the lesson? Don't rely on other people to tell you about a wardrobe malfunction, check it out for yourself, before you speak.

#72
Prepare to Laugh at Yourself

As the former example shows, things are going to happen that make you look foolish, and people are going to laugh at your blunders at times. Therefore, you have two choices. First, you can be offended, and let that destroy your presentation, and second, you can laugh with the audience, and make it part of the show. I recommend the latter.

Many years ago, I was playing music at a pub in rural Quebec. I was the lead guitar player in the band.

Because I was always prone to having bad things happen on the stage, I tried to be prepared as much as I could. Part of the preparedness was to have an extra guitar handy, because I broke guitar strings quite regularly.

It's always been important to me that the first song an audience hears us perform be an outstanding effort. You only make a first impression once, and I was almost anal about song selection to start off our set. I wanted the audience to hear us, and to love us, in the first ten seconds.

We took to the stage in the pub, which was absolutely packed. Our drummer counted in the first song, and with the strike of the first note, there was a loud "SPWAAAANG" as I broke a guitar string.

I took my guitar off and tried to put it down in order to grab the second guitar. Unfortunately, I was so upset about the opening song being ruined that I slammed the first guitar down into its stand too hard, and the extra force caused the stand to topple backward, where it hit one of the posts that held up our lights.

As the light post began to fall over, I had to grab it and stop it from going down, which made the start of our set even more ridiculous. I could hear the audience howling with laughter as they watched this very angry little man throwing guitars around, then struggling to keep the stage lights from crashing, all in the first ten seconds of the show.

I looked into the audience and saw them laughing, then I looked back at the band members, and saw them laughing too, so I couldn't help myself from changing my anger to laughter as well. Our show never did recover well that night, not only because of the awkward opening set, but because we were a crappy band to begin with. Nevertheless, once I learned to laugh at myself, life became far easier on the stage. This applies to any type of performance, including speaking.

So, what's the lesson? Things are going to happen that will throw you off your game. Learn to laugh at yourself; it'll make your life far more enjoyable.

Points to Ponder

1. Remember to review your notes before you go on

2. What are some great opening lines that are easy to remember and will capture attention in the first ten seconds?

3. Prepare this checklist and have it with you during your quiet-time before you speak:

    a. Do your face stretches

    b. Loosen up your voice

    c. Adjust your mental and physical posture

    d. Check your zipper, dress and teeth

CHAPTER 9

TAKE THE STAGE

#73
Enter From the Audience's Left (Stage Right)

This method has its roots in stage acting. Some claim there's a difference in the way an audience feels about a character (and a speaker) based on whether they enter from the left or the right. One theory suggests that entering from the audience's left makes an audience more comfortable because they read from left to right. This would apply, of course, only to audiences who do read from left to right.

The extension of this theory is that when you enter from the audience's left (stage right) you should exit to the audience's right (stage left) because our perception is that when characters leave the stage to our right (stage left), they're moving off into the distance and they're gone.

Some claim that when characters enter from the audience's left (stage right) they're seen as "good guys," but "bad guys" enter from the right (stage left).

I've read from several sources who suggest this tradition began with Shakespeare, though I haven't been able to find any scientific information to support this theory. It does, however, have a ring of truth to it in my mind, so I thought it was worthy of space in this book.

When I speak, I try to enter from the audience's left if I can, just in case there's actual merit to this theory. I wouldn't want my audience thinking I'm the "bad guy" as soon as I walk out onto the stage.

So, what's the lesson? You decide.

#74
Avoid the Apology

I would say the most common thing I see from my students is the tendency to walk up to the front, and tell us all the reasons why their talk is going to suck!

I haven't really prepared anything.

I'm not good at public speaking.

This isn't something I'd normally do.

I was going to talk about this other thing, but I changed my mind.

I didn't know I was going to be speaking today.

These are the most common opening statements I hear in my classes, and they're really just products of nervous energy. Most people are very uncomfortable with speaking in public, so when they walk up to the front to speak, they have to release that energy somehow. In their minds, what better way to do it than to explain to the audience members the reason they shouldn't expect too much? That takes the pressure off the speaker, right?

In actuality, these nervous opening statements make speaking more difficult, because they put you into a negative pattern right from the start. This means that something good has to happen in order to move you from a negative mindset and into a positive one, instead of you already being on a high note.

What you do or say on the way to the stage is critical, because your audience is forming an impression about you right from the start, even as you walk up and take your place front and center. What should you say on your way to the front? Nothing! When your name is called, you walk up to the front of the room, or onto the stage, sporting a huge smile, and step into the Spotlight like you own the place. Take your position in front of your audience, give them a moment to form their first impression of you, and then begin.

In the spring of 2010, I had the opportunity of being the motivational speaker at the 114th graduation ceremony of 'Willis College of Business and Technology' in Ottawa. There were between 500 and 600 people there, along with delegates, political figures and members of the press. I was sitting in the front row while I awaited my time to speak, but the front row was about fifty feet from the stage. Between the front row and the stage was quite an expanse of floor, lots and lots of floor.

The room was set up this way because some ceremonial activities had been conducted in that open floor space a little earlier in the day. This meant that when they introduced me, the walk to the stage felt like I was walking down the hall to the gas chamber.

I was only half-way to the stage by the time the applause generated by my introduction had ended. This left me with a walk of twenty-five feet or so to reach the short stairs, to climb up to the stage level, and to get across the stage, where the podium awaited me. I had to complete this trek in a rather uncomfortably silent room. Believe me, that's a long walk in front of such a large crowd.

A simple walk to a platform, to the front of a room, or to the center of a stage can be an ominous walk. The distance can seem overwhelming, and if there's a complete silence, it can be absolutely painful. But remember, as a speaker, anything you say during that walk is more likely to hurt you than help you, therefore, say nothing.

So, what's the lesson? Walk to the stage, the podium or to the front of the room like you own the place, and say nothing until you're ready to begin your talk.

#75
Avoid the Ramp-Up

The ramp-up is a very common tendency, especially among novice speakers. The ramp-up is best described as the urge to make nervous statements, a mistake many speakers commit when they first take the stage, something they do in order to get themselves into mental position. This is where the opening joke usually comes in, but, unless you're a comedian, this should be avoided, as previously discussed.

A ramp-up is an opening sequence that has less to do with your presentation, but more to do with trying to get your audience to like you, often by lightening the mood. The reality is that when you ramp-up, you're really trying to get your audience to like you by lightening up your own mood. It has nothing to do with the audience and everything to do with your own comfort level.

Phrases such as, "What a great looking audience," and, "I'm so happy to be here," and, "Today, I'm going to talk about…" are ramp-up lines. They really add no value to the presentation, and shouldn't be used in your opening statements.

I'm often asked, "Shouldn't we express our gratitude for the opportunity, and thank our host?" Yes, you should express gratitude and thanks, but do so either at the end of the presentation, or in the middle of it, if there's an appropriate and opportune time. Remember that you have about ten seconds to grab your audience's attention, and thanking your host and expressing your joy for the opportunity doesn't accomplish that task.

It's important to know precisely what you're going to say when you first open your mouth on the stage. Use an opening line that grabs the audience's attention. Here are a few good opening lines that I've heard:

I recently paid $135,000 for a dog.

Put up your hand if you plan on writing a book this weekend.

I have to tell you this story...

There will be roughly one-million presentations made today, and all but one of them will suck!

So, what's the lesson? Get right to your attention-getter, and grab the audience in the first ten seconds.

#76
Make Eye Contact and Nod

Make eye contact with your audience whenever you can.

In most speaking situations, you'll be able to see your audience members. So, take advantage of the opportunity to make them feel like you're speaking directly to them by making eye contact with them individually, just for a few seconds. As you make eye contact with someone, nod your head slightly if your message warrants it, and you'll notice their head begin to nod back. I've seen this a thousand times while speaking to smaller groups.

Of course, you want to avoid the over-exaggerated, manipulative bobbing of the head to enforce agreement. I'm suggesting a very slight nod to garner a mirrored response. This helps bring your audience into a state of agreement with you. It's subtle, but it works.

By making direct eye contact, you're not only engaging that audience member into your presentation, but you're also winning some trust. People tend to trust you more if you're willing to look them in the eye.

At the same time, you'll be able to spot those faces that offer you a welcoming or agreeable expression. Those faces can help you calm your nerves if you feel a little nervous all of a sudden.

Be sure to distribute your eye contact randomly throughout the audience. Oftentimes, I'll see a speaker at my events who'll focus in on me, and avoid the audience altogether. Sometimes, a speaker will have a favorite side of the room, and concentrate their connection with the audience in that one area.

Remember, your entire audience wants to connect with you on an individual basis, so make every attempt to offer that opportunity to as many audience members as you can. Scout the room and make eye contact for about five seconds with different individuals, in a random pattern of distribution. Do this while nodding your head a little to gain their agreement, and you can win an audience over, one member at a time.

So, what's the lesson? Making eye contact while slightly nodding your head can help you win over an entire audience.

#77
Step Away From the Podium

It's not always possible to step away from the podium. If you're delivering a formal speech, or hosting an awards show where there are cameras and Teleprompters, the podium can be your only option. But, if you do have the option, get out from behind the podium.

When you stand clear of the podium, it opens up your mid-section to the audience. When you become more open and available to your audience, you're essentially inviting them into your world. Because you're presenting yourself in a somewhat vulnerable state, without the protection of the podium, there's an unconscious feeling of trust that initially comes over your audience. Until you step out from behind the podium, your audience doesn't really know whether they can trust you or not. This isn't a conscious thought, necessarily; it's more of an unconscious response.

Once, a speaker began her talk from behind the podium, and then, after only a few minutes, stepped out from behind the podium and walked to the front of the stage. In this case, I found her approach highly effective. She began in a safe position behind the podium, so as not to overwhelm her audience with her presence. She was able to garner trust by virtue of her voice, her demeanor, and her message. When she came out from behind the podium, it was like giving the audience a message that she now trusted us, that we were her friends, having an intimate conversation. It was very powerful.

Being outside the confines of the podium also provides you with a world of expressive freedom not found otherwise. The podium restricts your movements, your gesturing and your ability to fully express your message.

When you walk onto the open stage, you have space in which to express yourself fully and engage your audience. All barriers are gone, and you can be whoever you want to be, in order to get your message across.

A podium is typically associated with a formal speech, in which information is transferred. The open stage is where authentic self-expression, and the transference of feeling and energy, takes place. That's where magic happens!

So, what's the lesson? Use your discernment regarding the podium, but I encourage you to make every effort to step away from it. Open yourself up to your audience, so you can invite each other into your respective worlds.

#78
Speaking With Gestures

What should you do with those awkward appendages when you have to speak in public? I'm referring, of course, to your hands. There's so much that can be said about this topic that Mark Bowden has written an entire book about it! (See his book, *Winning Body Language*.)

I used to get very frustrated when I was working with a specific training company, because they kept trying to get me to keep my hands down by my sides when I spoke. It was never comfortable for me to hang my hands down by my sides and to keep them there. Later, when I began offering my own training programs, I'd tell my students to let their hands go wherever they felt they needed to go naturally. It wasn't until I read Bowden's book that it all made sense! Your hands are not meant to dangle down by your sides unless you're in motion. Here are a few tips taken from Bowden's book that might help you.

There are different physical levels of gesturing, each with their own meaning. Two very powerful levels are what Bowden refers to as the TruthPlane and the PassionPlane.

The TruthPlane is the horizontal plane at the level of the navel. Gesturing with your hands at this level offers the audience a message that you are here to give, rather than to take away. Gesturing at this level garners trust.

The PassionPlane is the horizontal plane at the level of the heart. Gesturing at this level expresses an emotional attachment to your message. This is how you transfer feeling in your presentation.

An effective balance between the TruthPlane and the Passion-Plane levels of gesturing can significantly increase the impact of your message.

Here is a real, live example of how powerful these gesture planes can be:

In one of my events, with absolutely no preliminary explanation, I conducted an experiment. I asked for a volunteer to step in front of the audience and follow my very specific instructions. Her task was to hold her hands down by her sides (Bowden calls this the GrotesquePlane.) I asked her to say the following words in whatever natural tone she felt, "I've told you everything I know."

I then asked the audience to write down the first thought that came to their minds about the speaker's message.

I then asked the speaker to gesture at the TruthPlane, and to repeat the same words in whatever natural tone felt right. Interestingly enough, her entire tone changed, just by virtue of the fact that her hands were at a different level. I asked the audience to note their immediate response.

Next, we went to the PassionPlane. The same words were spoken, and once again, I saw a drastic change in the tone of the words. The audience noted their response.

Later, when I polled the audience, it was clear that the speaker's believability was highest when gesturing at the TruthPlane, was moderate at the PassionPlane, and was very low at the Grotesque-Plane. This experiment actually included all the other planes as well, including the DisclosurePlane (level of the mouth), the ThoughtPlane (level of the head) and the EcstasyPlane (above the head.) The speaker appeared to give a completely different message, using the exact same words, based only on the level of gesturing.

So, what's the lesson? The level at which you gesture can significantly change your intended message.

#79
Pockets or No Pockets?

This is going to make most speaking trainers roll their eyes in disagreement. So be it.

I was always taught to keep my hands out of my pockets when I speak. I was taught this, and I've seen this taught, through videos, through online software and through the classroom. The teaching was that a speaker should never put their hands in their pockets when they speak. I have but one word for that theory, "Rubbish!"

I was working for a large training organization that was adamant that my hands should never be in my pockets. I disagreed, so I went online to find evidence. As you can imagine, I found countless pictures of all the greatest speakers in the world with their hands in their pockets.

Here's the thing about having your hands in your pockets. For many, it's a protection mechanism. Many speakers will put their hands in their pockets, only because they don't know what else to do with them. In those cases, it LOOKS like a protection mechanism and, therefore, distracts the audience from the speaker's message. In those cases, I would agree; the hands shouldn't be in the pockets. However, many speakers put their hands in their pockets, not because it's a protection mechanism, but because it's comfortable, and when done smoothly, it gives off an air of coolness and self-assuredness. Go online and search for pictures of great speakers such as Zig Ziglar, Tony Robbins, and Bill Clinton, and you'll find pictures of each of them on the stage, with their hands in their pockets.

One thing to be aware of, however, is to make sure you have nothing in your pockets at the time. No change, no keys, no paper, or anything else. If you do have something in your pockets, you'll likely start fiddling with it and THAT can provide an undesirable impression on your audience.

There are two other things to note about using your pockets. Using only one hand is ordinarily best, and only for a short time. Make sure the use of your pockets doesn't hinder your gesturing. You need both hands to create the maximum impact with your gestures.

So, what's the lesson? If it's natural, and your pockets are empty, go ahead and use them, but with one hand only, and only for a short time.

#80
Don't Just Play the Notes, Play the Music

A friend of mine is a piano teacher. She teaches students of all ages and all skill levels. One of her students is a teenage prodigy named Jordon.

At a recital back in 2011, I sat in the front row and Jordon was performing an original piece of music. I was captivated by this young man's music, but even more so by his physical representation of it.

As he played, Jordon's eyes were closed. His hands floated over the keys, as if they were gliding on butter. His body moved with the tempo, his head swayed with the rhythm, and his facial expression clearly displayed what he was feeling as his own music came to life.

When the music became very quiet and mellow, Jordon's head dropped close to the keys as if he was listening to the sound of each individual key being pressed. He moved slowly and gracefully with the sound.

Then his back straightened, his eyes opened wide, and his face contorted into an expression of intensity as the crescendo built and the climax struck.

The music slowed down once again, and his head went down close to his hands again. As he reached the closing notes of his work, he let his right hand drift past the end of the piano and into the air as if to whisk the music off to heaven.

A long silence followed as Jordon slowly stood to take his bow. The audience began to rouse from the musical trance in which they had been locked, and, to a standing ovation, young Jordon claimed his accolades.

Any musician will tell you there are those who can play the notes, and those who can play the music. As a speaker, you need to say more than the words; you need to live the message. Your message to your audience isn't in your words; it's in your heart. Open your heart, free your authentic self, and get lost in your message, just like Jordon got lost in his.

So, what's the lesson? When you're speaking, play more than the notes. Play the music!

#81
Don't Speak to Your Audience, Converse With Them Instead

Wikipedia defines a conversation as, "communication between two or more people." A conversation flows two ways, and it should do so from the stage as well. Now, that doesn't mean both parties must speak; it means there's some communication between the two. This typically requires mutual attention and respect, in order to establish transference of both information, and emotion.

In order for you to converse with your audience, you first need their attention. A very simple way to command your audience's attention as soon as you take the stage is by giving them your attention first. You can do this through silence. That's right, say nothing, do nothing. Just stand there, and look into your audience. This lets your audience know they have your attention, and that you're expecting theirs. I've done this hundreds of times, and it works very well. It sometimes takes longer than is comfortable, but it does work, and you need to remain steadfast until you have everyone's attention, not just some of them.

If you begin speaking before you have your audience's attention, you're not conversing with them, you're merely speaking at them, and they're not listening.

Standing in silence and looking at your audience takes moxie, no doubt about it. But it can be a very powerful way to command their attention.

Once you have their attention, you'll need to gain their respect. You can do that by first giving them yours. Respect your audience by being properly prepared, appropriately dressed, professionally poised and effectively projected in your voice. The more prepared you are in every aspect of your presentation, the more respect you'll have shown for your audience, and the more respect they're likely to have for you.

With your audience's attention and respect, you're in a great position to just chat with them as you would a close friend, and they're in a position to do more than receive your message. They become silent participants in the conversation.

So, what's the lesson? Command your audience's attention, and respect, by first giving them yours, then just converse with them like you would with an old friend.

Points to Ponder

1. Reflect on your recent presentations. Did you "ramp up"? If so, take notice of that and make a mental note to avoid the ramp-up.

2. How has your eye contact been when you speak? Make a conscious decision to distribute your eye contact evenly throughout your audience.

3. Consider video-taping your next presentation and ask these questions when reviewing the video:

   a. Does the podium adversely affect your connection to your audience?

   b. Do your gestures support your message or detract from it?

   c. Do I look nervous?

   d. Am I playing the music or just the notes?

   e. Am I speaking at my audience or am I conversing with them?

CHAPTER 10

Gaining and Keeping Momentum

#82
How to Completely Kill the Moment

Imagine you're making love. You're in the middle of the steamiest moment. You're excited, engaged and completely involved, when all of a sudden, your partner stops, flips the page in the manual, reads the instructions, and then tries to pick up where he or she left off. Don't you just hate it when that happens?

I get so frustrated when a speaker has my attention, and is on a roll with a captivating message. When the speaker has me enthralled, both mentally and emotionally, but then has to stop to check notes. What a way to completely kill the moment!

Here's how you can prevent such a showstopper. Instead of notes or a script, consider using a mental picture stack.

In my training programs, the first thing I do is give my students a very simple mental picture to follow for their first presentation, and here it is:

In your mind, picture a huge name plate with your name on it, and picture it balancing on edge on the top of your head. You struggle to keep it balanced as it sways to and fro, but you manage to keep it balanced on your head.

At the same time, there's a rolled up map being stuffed up your nose, as if by some magical force. With your right hand you're trying to pull the map out of your nose, but it keeps pushing itself back in there.

While all of that's happening, there's a giant Cheerio stuck to your bottom lip, and it's pulling your bottom lip down. It's very heavy, and it's pulling your face down while you're trying to keep that map out of your nose, and you still have to keep balancing that name plate on your head.

As if that's not enough, your left hand's holding a goal net, like the ones used in ice hockey. This net is in front of your stomach, and it's very heavy, plus very awkward. Your left arm's tired from the weight of this goal net, your face is being pulled down by a giant Cheerio on your bottom lip, your right hand's fighting with the map that's pushing its way up your nose, and that name plate's still trying to fall off your head.

What on Earth could all of that possibly mean? It's a visual roadmap for the first presentation my students give in class. Their first assignment is to stand in front of the class, and tell us their name (name plate), where they're from (rolled up map), what their occupation is (Cheerio is "O" for occupation), and what their goal is in the class (goal net). See how that works?

This same process can be used for a presentation of any length of time, and it can completely remove the need for written notes. When it's time to move from one topic to the next, a moment of silent thought is all that's required to think about the next picture in the stack, and then to move into that topic. Your audience has no clue that you're using the notes, because they're in your mind.

The key to success in using this strategy is to exaggerate the pictures, and include motion. The more ridiculous the scenes, the easier it'll be to recall them. I've done entire workshops with this method. There's no limit to the number of items that you can recall, with a little practice.

So, what's the lesson? To keep the momentum going, get rid of the paper notes, and use picture stacks in your mind instead.

#83
Stay Within Your Time Limit. Always!

About thirty minutes before I began writing this section, I received a phone call from a friend who was scheduled to give a presentation that very evening. She asked me for some input on a few things. She shared with me that she'd been allocated five minutes for her presentation, but planned to "hijack" more time. I strongly advised against it, and I hope she heeded my advice. You'll have to buy the next book to find out if she did or not.

In late 2007 I held a seminar. As part of my session, I invited two guest speakers, both of them doctors.

Before the event, I spoke directly with each of them, and we discussed their allotment of time, and their main topics. We reached an agreement on topics, and on a fifteen-minute time limit. I planned the session, in significant part, around the agreed-upon topics and time limits.

During the session, the time came up for the first guest speaker to take the stage. His presentation was outstanding! As he presented, I sat off to one side of the platform, beside his laptop computer. He had to walk over to the computer many times, in order to advance his slides.

After his allotted fifteen minutes, there was no sign of his presentation coming near an end. After twenty minutes had passed, I flagged him down when he walked over to advance his slides. "Hey Doc, you have to wrap it up," I told him. He didn't, and I signaled for him to end about a dozen times.

After forty-five minutes, he finally ended his presentation, so I walked out onto the stage and politely thanked him. For the past half-hour, the second guest speaker had been standing there, ready to present, but his allotted time was already long gone as well.

I felt that we had to honor our invitation to the second guest speaker, so I introduced him, and welcomed him to the stage.

He, too, had agreed on a fifteen minute maximum, but took a full thirty minutes to complete his presentation.

The net result was that I wasn't able to include all of the information I had planned for the seminar. The complete second half of the seminar was destroyed, because I wasn't able to squeeze it all in.

I learned two important lessons that day. The first lesson was that I won't allow a guest speaker to hijack my meetings again. The next time, I'll walk right out onto the stage if I must and wrap their presentation up for them. The second lesson I learned was that I'll never do that to anyone else. Never will I run overtime in a presentation. It's disrespectful to the organizers, to all of the other speakers who must follow, and to the audience.

So, what's the lesson? Be respectful; always stay within your allocated time limit.

#84
Use Flip Charts Backwards

This is a cool little trick I learned years ago.

You've probably seen presenters struggle with the flip chart paper, as they try to lift it over the top of the chart. The paper gets crumpled, and won't fall properly. Most speakers have struggled with this, from time to time.

When I use a flip chart, I turn all of the pages up first, so that I begin using the last page of the pad, and I flip them from back to front. I do this for two reasons:

First, when the pages are flipped over the top of the chart, it's much easier to grab them from behind the chart. The pages are already separated, and they're at chest height, so I don't have to bend down.

Second, once I grab the sheet, there's already a forward pulling force on it, because the sheets are mounted on the front of the chart, and the fold is pulling the paper for me. I simply have to lift the sheet a little, and let gravity drop it smoothly into place.

Try it! Flip the papers of the flip chart backwards, from back to front. You'll see how smoothly you can flow through those pages, with next to zero effort, and no awkward fumbles.

So, what's the lesson? I think you get it!

#85
Whatever Happens, Make It Look Deliberate

In early summer of 2010, my daughter graduated from high school. I was sitting in an auditorium that held maybe a thousand people or more, and I was enjoying the very elaborate graduation ceremony. The valedictorian was scheduled to give his speech in a few minutes, but, before he got to do so, the power went out in the auditorium. The entire stage went black, and the sound system shut off, so nothing worked anymore. The emergency lights came on, but they were positioned to illuminate the exits, not the stage.

Now, if you're a seventeen-year-old, about to give your speech as the class valedictorian, is this not pretty much the highlight of your life up to this point? Does this not rank up there as one of the most important events in your life so far? I wonder what must have gone through his mind, as his time to make his speech approached, and he had no light from which to read his speech, and no sound system with which to project his voice. I can only imagine the anxiety that must have been surging through him.

The Master of Ceremonies had to keep the program going, so, with a loud, booming voice, the MC introduced the valedictorian, whom no one could see in the dark.

This young man stepped to the front of the stage, where there was a single ray of very dim light from one of the emergency lights, and, from memory, he began to speak. The entire auditorium went completely silent, as we strained to hear the young man's voice, but we only had to strain for a moment. As the crowd fell silent in the auditorium, his voice rang through the stands as clearly, and with as much professionalism, as I've ever heard from a speaker.

He had no light, had no script, and had no microphone. Yet, he captured the attention of every person in the auditorium, all thousand-plus of us. His speech was profound, was masterfully delivered, and was one of the best speeches I can remember being a witness to. It was like he'd planned it this way all along. Two minutes after his speech ended, the power came back on, but he had already won us over in the dark.

I have to tell you another story, because it fits in so well with this topic.

A close friend of mine is a master magician, and his name is Elliott Smith. In late summer of 2010, while Elliott was performing in a magic show, there was suddenly an earthquake. In Ottawa, Canada, earthquakes aren't common. This one happened to hit in the middle of Elliott's show. He briefly stopped his performance and waited for the tremor to stop, then looked at his audience and, without skipping a beat, asked, "Now, who wants to see me do that again?"

So, what's the lesson? Expect the unexpected. When it happens, make it look like it was all part of the plan.

#86
Have Fun

This is the simplest, but pretty much the most important, of all the rules of speaking in public.

When I was in the band, I used to say that our audience will never get more excited about our music than we will.

For years, our band traveled the country, playing every kind of venue you can think of. We sold out at pubs and taverns, we broke attendance records in some venues, and we even had a fan club. The funny thing about this is that we weren't that good of a band! Our music was fine, but not nearly as good as many other bands. We weren't as polished as many other bands, plus we didn't have the best equipment on the planet. I believe we just weren't as talented as many other bands, but they weren't doing nearly as well as we were. So, what was our secret? We were fun!

We had more fun on that stage than any other band touring around, during that time period. We made jokes, we screwed up regularly on stage, we laughed at each other, we jumped around, and we had loads and loads of fun every single time we hit the stage, but every second of it was sincere and honest. We just loved to be in front of an audience, and it showed. The result was that we had people flocking in to come and see us play.

The exact same concept holds true for speakers. Some speakers don't seem to appreciate the magnitude of the opportunity, or the responsibility they've been given by being on the stage. The Spotlight is glorious, and we, as speakers, should respect it, we should savor it and most of all, we should enjoy it.

The worst thing a speaker can do to an audience is to bore them. An audience will forgive just about any mishap, any mistake, or any fumble, as long as they're having a good time. There's no way an audience is going to have a good time, if the speaker isn't also.

I'm not suggesting that you need to jump around like an idiot on the stage. We did that in the band at times, because it was fitting of the environment we were in. I'm simply suggesting that your audience will never elevate themselves beyond your emotional elevation. While you're on stage, you're the leader. Your audience looks to you to establish the emotional altitude.

So, what's the lesson? Above all else, have fun. Your audience will love you for it!

#87
Share the Stage, But Be Careful

On occasion, I like to share the stage. I'll bring up a volunteer to participate in a demonstration, or even bring up a guest to share a quick story. This can be very effective, but also very dangerous, and you'll need to decide for yourself how adventurous you want to get.

In item #83, I explained the importance of staying within your time limit. If you plan to share the stage, you'll need to make sure your guest agrees to, and abides by, a time limit, or you may have to politely interject, and stop them from taking over your program.

Another risk is that your guest may not behave exactly according to plan. I invited a volunteer to the stage once, and, to prove a point, set up a scenario that was meant to garner a specific reaction from the volunteer. This scenario had him walking down the street, and had him see me coming toward him. He was to recognize me as his long-lost brother. He was to have been searching for me all of his life, and right out of the blue, there I was. I asked him how he would respond. I expected him to open his arms, and to welcome his long-lost brother back into his life, but instead, this volunteer put his hands on his hips, and yelled angrily, "Where the hell have you been?" Not exactly the response I was hoping for.

So, what's the lesson? Sharing the stage can get a laugh, and it can enhance the experience for your audience, as well as help you prove a point. Be aware, however, that it can also be fraught with peril. Be prepared for the possibility that things might not develop the way you expected them to.

#88
Audience Engagement

I recently attended a workshop, conducted by an experienced professional speaker. As part of the session, we were all given an opportunity to deliver a short presentation. My presentation included a bit of audience interaction. After I completed my presentation, our host strongly suggested that, as speakers, we should never engage our audience. His argument was that we relinquish control when we do this, and may find it difficult to get that control back.

I have to tell you, I have over thirty years of experience, having been in the entertainment business, and in the speaking business, and I would beg to differ. I engage my audience at every opportunity. Though it does require some skill to maintain control at times, the rewards are well worth whatever risk is present.

Your audience members don't want to be static recipients of your message. They want to be a part of the show. That doesn't mean you should be getting them on the stage, although that can, and should, happen occasionally. It does mean, however, that they want to be, at the very least, mentally and emotionally involved.

There are safe ways to engage your audience and still maintain control. For example, you can have them raise their hands, have them stand up, have them yell out answers to your questions, or even have them catch things you toss out to them, always in a safe fashion, obviously! These are very simple ways to engage your audience, and it takes nothing away from your performance, but it brings your audience into the game with you.

There is one stipulation that should be noted, however. Audience engagement must have a purpose, other than to get them engaged. There must be a reason for getting them to do something. Otherwise, it comes across as a tactic, and not an important part of the session. If you're going to ask for them to raise their hands, do something with that resulting show of hands. Explain the purpose of the exercise. Have a point to it all.

I've seen many speakers ask their audience to interact, with no explanation or reason behind the interaction. This gets old very fast, and your audience will stop complying, or comply out of politeness, and begrudge you every minute of it.

So, what's the lesson? Get your audience engaged, but with a purpose in mind, and you'll keep their attention.

#89
Asking Questions, What's the Point?

I was watching a motivational speaker do a session about finances. This speaker was a little too hyper for my taste, but he did do a good job of keeping my attention. He was loud, he was fast, and he was big on the stage. Every time he made a point, he'd hold his right hand straight up in the air, and he'd ask, "True, or true?" He'd then move over to his next point immediately.

In this particular case, he was clearly asking the question rhetorically, and his audience recognized that. It was a presentation tactic, because he really gave his audience no way to disagree, so this was just a little quirk that he included in his presentation, to make himself a little different from the rest of the speakers, and I must say it worked. I remembered him, and I'm writing about him right now.

However, I've seen too many speakers pose questions to their audience, and really give no chance for the audience to respond to the question, or, if the audience does get a chance to respond, there's nothing done with that response information.

Let's explore a few tips to help you be more effective at engaging your audience when asking questions.

First, only ask a question if you know the answer, or if an unexpected answer won't disrupt your presentation. The next item, point #90, provides a great explanation for this.

Second, make sure your audience knows how to give you the answer. Give clear instructions, in order to avoid confusion. For example, asking, "Have you ever had to stand on your head?" doesn't provide clear instructions on giving a response. Instead, if you give the audience this task, "Put your hand up if you've ever had to stand on your head," it provides clear instructions on what's expected as a response. Hands will either go up, or they won't, and either way, you've been provided with a response.

Third, have a reason for asking for a response, and do something with the response. You could say, "Put your hand up if you've ever had to stand on your head." And then, you could follow that up with, "I see that less than half the room has ever had to stand on their head. This shows that..." In this way, you've asked the audience for information, and your audience now knows why you wanted that information. They know the reason they either raised their hands or not.

So, what's the lesson? Ask questions of your audience only if you have good reason to, and explain what that reason is, but also give clear instructions on how they're to respond.

#90
If You Don't Know the Answer,
Don't Ask the Question

Around 1987, I was sitting in a large conference room that held between eighty and one-hundred other business people. Our host was at the podium, introducing our guest speaker. The guest speaker had just published a new book. He was the founder of an organization and on the board of directors for another corporation. He had a list of credentials a mile long.

As his name was announced, our guest speaker stepped up to the podium. As I watched him, I noticed how successful he looked. He was tall, confident, and self-assured. He was wearing an expensive looking suit that was most likely custom tailored, and I was thinking, "This is going to be really good!"

As our speaker stepped up to the podium, he raised his right hand high into the air, and he asked this question, "By a show of hands, who here has read *The One Minute Manager*?" (This wasn't the book this speaker had written.)

I hadn't read that book, so I didn't raise my hand. I look around the room, and not a single hand was raised.

"No one has read, *The One Minute Manager*?" he asked, now looking a little concerned. I scanned the room again, and still found no hands in the raised position.

Our speaker began to stumble over his words at this point, as if he'd been completely thrown off by the fact that nobody in the room had read that book. He grabbed a piece of paper off the podium, and his hand began to shake so badly we could hear that paper rattle clear across the room. After a few seconds of stumbling and stammering, our speaker took both of his hands, brought them up to his face, and began to weep like a child.

My jaw dropped, and I was now staring at this man in complete disbelief. I figured this must be part of his show, or something of the kind. After a few moments, he removed his hands from his face; he then wiped his hands on his custom tailored suit, as he picked up his papers and he walked out the door.

Our speaker didn't anticipate the answer to his question would be anything other than what he was prepared for. When he was caught off guard by the audience response, it threw him right off his game, and everything in his mind came crashing down around him. To this day, I don't recall this poor man's name, nor have I seen him anywhere else since.

So, what's the lesson? Never pose a question to an audience, unless you either know what their answer will be in advance, or you're thoroughly prepared to handle any other possible answer that could come up.

Points to Ponder

1. Review your notes before your next presentation. Are they so long that you will have check with them during your presentation or are they just keywords that you can see at a glance?

2. Do you typically sun over your allocated time? If so, make a personal commitment to stay within your time limit at every engagement.

3. Think about your last few times on stage. Did you have fun? Did your audience?

4. Give some serious thought as to how you will engage your audience the next time you speak.

5. Practice asking questions in such a way that:

   a. your audience knows exactly how to respond

   b. you have a purpose for asking the question and a use for the answer

   c. you know exactly what to do next with whatever answer your get, even if it's an answer you don't expect

CHAPTER 11

Being Sensational

#91
Write Your Own Introduction

How you're introduced to an audience is the first step to being sensational on the stage. The introduction is a critical point in your presentation, because it's your audience's first exposure to you. You want it to be perfect! Don't waste this precious opportunity, an opportunity that lets you paint a picture in your audience's mind about who you are. Leaving your introduction to the discretion of the Master of Ceremonies isn't going to give you the powerful opening you need. Unfortunately, many speakers omit this important step.

To write an effective introduction, spare the audience from having to endure a long and painful list of your accomplishments. They don't really care about what you've done that much. It's always best to keep your introduction short, sweet, and powerful. Include only the information that's really important to your audience, and use your introduction as a mood-setter.

At one of my recent events, I had the privilege of introducing Peggy McColl, a *New York Times* Best-Selling Author. You've already read about her in this book.

Peggy has a list of accomplishments that could go on forever, and I could probably spend an entire twenty-minute presentation just rattling off her past work. At our session, however, the topic she was to present her advice about was how to write a book in a single weekend. Peggy didn't send me an introduction, so I formulated my own. (I bet she won't do that again, after she reads this book!)

Even though I could have gone on and on about how amazing she is, I restricted her introduction to three relevant points:

1. She's a *New York Times* best-selling author, and this establishes respect for her work.

2. She's written eight books, and this establishes her vast wisdom and experience.

3. Her most recent book was written in a single weekend, and this proves she's just done what she's going to teach us to do.

Her introduction went something like this, "Our next speaker is a *New York Times* Best Selling Author. She recently completed her eighth book, which she wrote in a single weekend, and she's here today to show you how she did it, so you can do it too. Please help me welcome Peggy McColl."

This is a simple, but effective introduction. When you prepare your introduction, include only the credentials that are relevant to the situation. Make it short, make it sweet, and set yourself up so that your audience awaits your first word with baited breath.

So, what's the lesson? Take control of how you're looked upon, as you step onto the stage. Write your own introduction.

#92
Humor? You Must Be Joking!

About two weeks before writing this chapter, my step-son, Daniel, told me he was giving a presentation in one of his university courses. He told me he was planning on starting with a joke, because he was taught to begin presentations that way. Not by me, he wasn't!

The joke he planned to open with was lame, not at all funny, and very old. Is there a worse way to begin a presentation? Probably, but I've never seen it.

Unless you're a comedian, jokes have no place in presentations, or speaking gigs. Now, before you humorists get all up in arms, let me explain my reasoning. A joke and a humorous anecdote aren't the same things.

If you can pull off humor in a presentation, you're golden with your audience! But telling a canned joke is a very risky business. There are many reasons not to use canned jokes in your presentation, not the least of which is that your audience may have heard those jokes before. Your audience may not think your jokes are funny, or they may find your jokes offensive.

Humor, on the other hand, is a great way to keep your audience fully engaged. Humor should be spontaneous, or at least, appear to be so, and it should be directed at you. This is generally the safest way to interject humor, because you're less likely to offend if you're making fun of yourself.

Not everyone can effectively use humor in their speeches, and if you're one of those people, don't try to force it. Some people aren't naturally funny, and trying to be something you're not can kill your presentation.

So, what's the lesson? If you can pull it off, use seemingly spontaneous, self-directed humor. If you're not funny by nature, leave the humor to the humorists.

#93
Smile

Must I REALLY explain this one? Actually, it seems so!

It sounds like such a simple concept, but I have seen presenters walk to the stage completely stone-faced, and then try to warm up the audience with a joke.

Your presentation doesn't begin when you open your mouth, it begins the second you become visible to your audience. Before you even make it all the way to the stage much of your audience has already taken a good look at your face. They have already passed an initial judgment on you.

If your objective is to win your audience over, a smile will help make that happen. Be warm with your audience; show them that you're sincerely happy to be there with them.

So, what's the lesson? Smile!

#94
Speak Slower Than You Think Is Natural

I'm a very fast talker. The average English-speaking person speaks at about 120 words per minute. I suspect that I speak at about 150, with gusts up to about 225, when I get on a roll.

It's a natural tendency to speak faster when you're nervous, or excited. And a faster pace signals excitement or urgency, so it can be a good thing in some cases. More often, however, our pace can increase dramatically, and we're not aware of doing so.

To help you take control of your speaking pace, and to help you keep your verbal velocity more deliberate, record your talks and presentations. Listen to them carefully afterward, paying attention to your pacing. In addition, consider planting someone in the audience who can signal you when you're raging out of control.

For speakers whose pattern is to speak at a higher rate of speed, slowing ourselves down can feel painful and unnatural. If you're a fast talker, one way to flag yourself down is to embed a yield sign into your mental notes. As you may remember, keeping mental notes was the topic of Chapter Ten, Item #82. This gives you a mental reminder to be conscious of your speed, and to slow your pace down to a speed that may feel less than natural to you. If it feels uncomfortably slow to you, it's likely about right for the audience.

To this day, I run into this problem all the time. When I provide a webinar, or do a recording session, I post a sign that says, "SLOW DOWN," in big block letters, and I keep this sign on my wall or desk. I also record almost every presentation I give, so I can review them and further improve my delivery. In almost every presentation or talk I give, I find at least one occasion where I go off the rails with my pacing.

So, what's the lesson? If you're a fast talker, build in some flags to slow you down to a pace that might feel a little uncomfortable for you. That's probably the right pace for the audience.

#95
Learn The Rules,
Then Break Them. Carefully!

Knowing all the "rules" that are laid out in this book, as well as in many other great books about public speaking, is critically important. It's important to know these rules, in order for you to follow them, but also in order for you to break them!

Someone who has no training or knowledge about how to speak in public effectively will likely break every rule there is, and their presentation will be a mess. However, every now and then, we see amazing speakers who seem to break the rules so effectively that they make a huge impression.

At a conference in Atlanta, Georgia, I witnessed a speaker who looked so unpolished, and looked so rough around the edges, that my first impression was, "Who the heck is this character, and what's he doing on the stage?" His mastery of the stage was quickly apparent when he began to speak, however. This guy was brilliant, but he broke the rules of stage etiquette regularly, and that's what made him unique and memorable. He was foul-mouthed, and he cracked offensive jokes, but he was able to do it in such a way the audience just loved him for it.

I don't, for one second, recommend that you try to pull that off! This speaker was one of those rare individuals who could just do it. He had everyone in the place laughing hysterically, but when it came time to make his serious points, he was as professional and powerful as any speaker I've ever seen.

What worked for this speaker won't likely work for you, but there may be other rules you can think of breaking. You must be selective, and you must use caution in doing so, but if you do so successfully, it will help make you a little different than other speakers. As you review this book, consider which of the principles don't resonate well with your personality. Then go right ahead and break those principles. Be brave, be creative, and be ground-breaking, but do so with the objective of being a better speaker, not a lazy speaker.

So, what's the lesson? If you're going to break the rules, do it selectively and with caution, as long as it improves your performance.

#96
You Never Know Who's In the Audience

Always comport yourself as if the most important person in your life's watching you, because they may just be doing so!

I've often been told that so and so had been in the audience, after I've delivered a talk or a presentation. I've learned to comport myself as if the most important person in the world's watching me at all times, and I learned this lesson in Thunder Bay, Ontario, back in the early 1980's.

I was on the road with the band, and three of us headed to a Laundromat, to get our laundry done. We were always joking around, and making fun of ourselves, whether on the stage, or off the stage. The Laundromat was mostly empty, with the exception of the three of us, and one older man, who was sitting alone at the other end of the room, engrossed in his book.

We were all wearing our band jackets, with the name of the band, "Midnite Sun," emblazoned on the back, and with our individual names on the shoulders. We were goofing around, and making fun of each other, as was usually the case. Then I decided to give our agent a call from the pay phone, because we'd had a cancellation for the following week, and he was working on finding a replacement gig.

I spoke with him on the phone for a few minutes, and then announced to my band mates that after we were done in Thunder Bay, we were off to a place called Assiniboia, in Saskatchewan. Who'd ever heard of such a place? Certainly not us, and so we made jokes about the name, and how it must be a little hick town, along with all the other wisecracks that young men generate.

The next morning, the front page of the newspaper held a headline that read, "Midnite Sun En Route to Assiniboia." The page was split in two columns. The first column talked about our silly antics in the Laundromat, and the second column gave a short history about the town of Assiniboia, Saskatchewan.

The older gentleman in the Laundromat was a reporter, and he wasn't reading his book, he was writing in it. He had quoted some of our silly wisecracks, and explained how he'd enjoyed watching us have our fun in the Laundromat.

That evening, we broke the all-time attendance record at the venue we were performing in. There was a lineup of patrons wanting to get in, and it stretched out the door and down the street.

Similar events have happened to me many times over the years, so I've learned that you never know who's in the audience watching you, even when you're not on a stage.

So, what's the lesson? Always comport yourself as if the most important person in the world's watching, because they just might be!

#97
Lighten Up, Will Ya?

Holly is an amazing lady I have the good fortune of knowing! She's a former police officer, now turned entrepreneur, and she attended one of my public speaking classes the evening before I wrote this piece. Because of her training in interrogation techniques as a police officer, Holly tends to be a little rigid when she speaks. She has a fun and loveable personality, but when she stands before an audience, she turns into a bit of a drill sergeant.

Holly stood in front of the class, impeccably dressed with her suit jacket done up, just as it should be when she's speaking to an audience. Then, Holly the drill sergeant began to speak.

I asked her to undo her jacket button, just so she could feel a little less formal. She protested slightly, but she finally complied, and began to loosen up a little. As she was speaking, I had to interrupt her a few times, and ask for Holly the lady to speak, instead of Holly the drill sergeant.

Finally, after several interruptions, Holly the lady broke free. All of the sudden, there she was, the woman we'd all been waiting for. Holly the lady began to speak. She told us about an accident that had befallen her, when she was trapped in an elevator as it fell six stories to the ground. She finally became animated and emotional, and it was so powerful that she had us all captivated. She lightened up from her Holly the drill sergeant persona!

Holly has a little more work to do, because she slipped back into drill sergeant mode after she finished the story, but that's okay, because now she knows how to lighten up, and it's going to profoundly improve her speaking skills.

So, what's the lesson? Lighten up when you take the stage. Your audience will relate to you so much better if you're just being you.

#98
Stick Around.
People Will Want to be Close To You

Because of all the years I've spent speaking and performing, I've learned a lot of lessons about what to do to stand out from the crowd. One of those lessons is to stick around, after the show or presentation is over.

When we were on the road with the band, I noticed that many other bands would completely leave the place right after they finished performing, or even step out when they were on their breaks. Our band never did that. We always made ourselves available to the crowd. We didn't do this as some sort of strategy, we simply enjoyed the attention. People would flock around us! Most people love to speak with the someone that was on the stage, and that applies to speakers, as well as performers.

In the fall of 2010, I attended a conference, hosted by a large mortgage company. This event featured two excellent speakers. One of them left immediately after his presentation, while the other stayed, and he mingled with the audience for quite some time afterwards. Which one do you think people remember the most? Certainly, they remember the speaker who mingled, because people felt like they were able to get to know him a little.

Of course, it's not always possible to stay, especially if your schedule has you catching a flight, or you're scheduled to speak somewhere else. I mentioned that I try not to travel on the day that I speak. That applies to traveling to the gig, as well as from the gig. Wherever possible, if I'm speaking out of town, my intention is to schedule my time so that I have nowhere to go immediately after the gig, even if that means staying the night at a hotel. The connections that are often made after a speaking gig can be too valuable to pass up.

So, what's the lesson? Whenever feasible, schedule your time so that you can remain available to mingle after your presentation.

#99
Go Forth and Change the World!

If you have something to say, say it! Don't ever let someone else silence your voice. Tell your story, share your dreams and sing your song. The world needs what you carry inside you, and you have the opportunity to change lives with your words.

At every opportunity, take the stage, grab the Spotlight, and tell the world who you are, and what you believe in. Your wisdom could be the catalyst that ignites the fire within someone else, and this someone else could go on to change the world.

Remember, stories are meant to be told. The world is listening; all you have to do is speak!

Points to Ponder

1. Write an introduction for yourself and keep it handy.

2. Consider seriously whether or not humor is part of your personality, or do you have to force it?

3. Review a video of one of your recent talks.

    a. Are you smiling?

    b. How is your speed?

4. Which rules are you ready to break in a carefully planned, strategic manner? Will this enhance your presentation or damage it?

5. Consider your presence when you speak. Do you need to lighten up a little?

APPENDIX A

POWERPOINT TIPS

Sensational speakers speak from the soul, not from the screen. If you must use slides, such as PowerPoint, here are some tips:

TIP #1: Use PowerPoint, or other slides, only when it truly enhances your presentation. For each slide, ask yourself, "Does this slide actually fulfill a purpose, or is it just duplicating me?" If it's duplicating you, one of you is irrelevant. Get rid of it.

TIP #2: The text on your slides should never be less than 36 points in size. Any smaller, and your slides may not be recognizable to anyone more than a few rows from the front. Some people say 32 points is okay, but I've seen 32 point font get lost in the viewing. When it comes to the text on your PowerPoint slides, go big or go home.

TIP #3: There are many reasons to avoid bullet points. The human brain recognizes and remembers "gist" before "detail." When your presentation is full of bullet points, you're using detail to build gist, and this is completely opposite to how the brain works. Use large pictures, instead of text, and the retention factor jumps from 10% to 65% in most cases. (See page 234 of, *Brain Rules*, by Dr. John Medina).

TIP #4: Need another reason to avoid bullet points? Factor in that our brain accepts information using both an audio channel, and a visual channel. When we read words, our brain is using the AUDIO channel to convert those words into sound. If your audience is supposed to be listening to you speak, but they're also trying to read bullet points, the audio channel becomes crowded, and the visual channel isn't being used at all, substantially diluting the audience's attention.

TIP #5: Each slide should have only one purpose, one point, one image, and/or one caption. As a rule of thumb, and yes, there are exceptions, if you can't write your caption on a 3 x 3 inch sticky note, you have too many words for one slide. Your audience should be able to look at your slide and get the point in one second flat, then turn their attention back to you, the speaker, where it belongs.

TIP #6: Remove anything your slides contain that doesn't support your message. Things you should remove are logos, flashy backgrounds, borders, animations, and graphics that don't mean anything. Your slides will only do one of two things, support your message, or detract from your message. Do you really need a logo on every slide? Doesn't your audience already know who you are? Promote with your talent, not your slides.

TIP #7: PowerPoint has awesome animation tools. Use them wisely to build the story with your slides, never to simply dazzle your audience. With every animation, ask yourself this, "Does this support my message, or is it just here because it's cool?" If it's just there for the cool factor, dump it. If it enhances your point, keep it in there. Remember, YOU'RE the presentation, your slides are only there to enhance.

About the Author

Steve Lowell has been speaking and performing on the live stage since the age of 6; that's over 50 years ago.

From Ottawa, Canada, Steve is an award-winning, global speaker and for over 30 years he has been training and mentoring executives, thought-leaders and professional speakers around the world to deliver high-impact keynote speeches, drive revenue from the platform and build wealth through speaking.

He's the 2021 President of the Global Speakers Federation (GSF) and the past national President of the Canadian Association of Professional Speakers (CAPS) and the 2021 President of the Global Speakers Federation (GSF).

He is one of fewer than 12% of the world's professional speakers to hold the Certified Speaking Professional (CSP) designation; the highest designation in professional speaking. He shares the stage with such greats as Jack Canfield (*Chicken Soup for the Soul* Series), Kevin Harrington (*Shark Tank* and "As Seen on TV"), Grant Cardone (*The 10X Rule*) and Brian Tracy (Author of over 70 books).

Together with his wife Jayne, he travels the world speaking, training and mentoring those who have a message to monetize through the spoken word.

Want to Learn More?

Whenever you're ready... here are three ways we can help you design your 'Expert Insights" through your own "Deep Thought Strategy" to drive business without the pitch.

1. Register for our e-learning course and be a part of our global Facebook community
Our entry-level online training program is a superb start if you are wanting to get started on your own "Deep Thought Strategy". Begin by discovering your own "Expert Insights" at www.BigMoneyMessage.com

2. Join one of our Implementation Programs and be a Case Study
We offer small case study groups (maximum 6 participants) who learn how to craft and implement their "Expert Insights" and then become a case study to demonstrate the power of the 'Expert Insights" concepts. This is by application only. To apply, send an email to hello@thelowells.global with the subject "Case Study Group"

3. Work with Us Privately
If you'd like to work directly or privately with us to implement your "Deep Thought Strategy", just send us a message at hello@thelowells.global and with the word "Private"... tell us a little about your business and what you'd like to work on together, and we'll get you all the details!

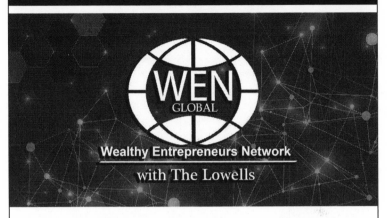

HEARTS to be HEARD

Giving a Voice to Creativity!

Your donation will give a voice to the creativity
that lies within the hearts of physically,
spiritually and mentally challenged children.

By helping us publish their books,
musical creations and works of art you will
make a difference in a child's life;
a child who would not otherwise be heard.

Donate now by going to
HeartstobeHeard.com

The children thank you!!